An Appeal to the U.S Supreme Court & A Proposal to Our President

Revised Edition

Pia Fields

An Appeal to the U.S Supreme Court & A Proposal to Our President
Copyright © 2025 by Pia Pikwah Fields

All rights reserved. No part of this publication may be reproduced, distributed, or transmitted in any form or by any means, including photocopying, recording, or other electronic or mechanical methods, without the prior written permission of the publisher or author, except in the case of brief quotations embodied in critical reviews and certain other noncommercial uses permitted by copyright law.

Although every precaution has been taken to verify the accuracy of the information contained herein, the author and publisher assume no responsibility for any errors or omissions. No liability is assumed for damages that may result from the use of information contained within.

Paperback: 979-8-9930791-3-4

Printed in the United States of America

CONTENTS

Foreword v

Additional Media vii

About This Case xix

Petition For Extraordinary Writ Of Certiorari Of Mandamus xxiix

Questions Presented xxx

List Of The Parties xxxi

Petition For A Writ Of Mandamus 1

Opinions Below 2

Rule 20 Statement 2

Statement Of The Case 4

Reasons For Granting The Writ 4

Conclusions 26

The Author's Proposal 35

Appendix Table Of Contents 40

Postscript 242

A Letter To The Chinese Consulate And Chinese Leaders 245

Afterword: Additional Resources From The Author 248

FOREWORD

In memory of Doctor Philip H. Groginsky, who risked his life to help the Fishman (Fields) family in 1918 when a Spanish flu killed twenty-one million people worldwide. He signed both a death certificate and a birth certificate for Sydney Fields, who was born one day after his father died.

One hundred years later, Sydney's ten-million-dollar assets were stolen by five nieces-in-law of his predeceased third wife. A will drafter made a sworn statement to support them and dismissed it later. He had no witnesses, no video and audio tapes to record his service for the 96-year-old blind testator. Yet, a judge accepted that "will" and created a tragedy in U.S. courtrooms.

The Fields family got nothing after spending one hundred thousand dollars in legal fees. However, they noticed and appreciated the love that Sydney had for his family. The tragedy that continued for one hundred years should be memorialized as well.

CERTIFIED TRANSCRIPT OF DEATH
STATE OF NEW YORK
DEPARTMENT OF HEALTH

NAME: Samuel Fishman

SEX: Male

DATE OF DEATH: December 29, 1918 **DISTRICT NO.:** 5254

PLACE OF DEATH: (Street & No.) N/A **INDEX NO.:** 69

DATE OF BIRTH: December 25, 1886 **AGE:** 32

PLACE OF BIRTH: Russia

SERVED IN US ARMED FORCES (Years)

MARITAL STATUS: Married **OCCUPATION:** Cattle Business

FATHER'S NAME: David Fishman

MOTHER'S MAIDEN NAME: Mollie Lichtman

CERTIFYING PHYSICIAN OR CORONER: Philip H. Groginsky, M.D.

MANNER OF DEATH: Pneumonia (Broncho) (Influenza)

FUNERAL HOME: N/A

PLACE OF BURIAL: Mountaindale

DATE FILED: December 30, 1918

This is to certify that the information concerning the death of the above named person is a true and accurate transcription of the information recorded on the original local certificate of death on file with the local registrar of ___Town of Fallsburg___, New York.
Name of Locality

Signature of Local Registrar
Elizabeth Malaro-Santos - DeputyClerk
DATE February 7, 2020

Do not accept this transcript unless the raised seal of the issuing locality is affixed thereon.
Any Alteration Invalidates This Certificate
See Reverse Side For A List of Security Features Used In This Form

DOH-4144 (6/2002)

SEE REVERSE SIDE FOR LIST OF SECURITY FEATURES

Birth Certificate on Dec. 30th, 1918

SCHEDULE 6 TO APPLICATION FOR PRELIMINARY LETTERS TESTAMENTARY
PROBATE PROCEEDING, WILL OF SYDNEY H. FIELDS, FILE # 2016-111
(Estimated Date of Death Valuations)

Bank and Brokerage Accounts

Merrill Edge	$	29,025
Popular Community IRA	$	183,063
Popular Community – xxx 0464	$	5,053
NY'S 529	$	20,858
Deutsche Asset & Wealth Mgt.	$	31,307
Chase Checking – xxx 7071	$	25,687
Chase Checking – xxx 9065	$	92,873
Comcast Stock	$	22,719
Vangard 1	$	4,165,408
Vangard 2	$	1,811,750
Vangard 3	$	1,564,352
Total:	$	7,929,386

STATE OF NEW YORK
SURROGATE'S COURT: COUNTY OF NEW YORK

PROBATE PROCEEDING
WILL OF SYDNEY H. FIELDS

a/k/a

Deceased.

APPLICATION FOR
PRELIMINARY LETTERS TESTAMENTARY
(See SCPA 1412)

New York County Surrogate's Court
PROBATE DEPT.
JUN 0 6 2016
FILED

File # 2016-111

1. The proposed preliminary executor (s) is/are DIANA PALMERI
and is/are designated as executor (s) in the Will of the above named decedent dated October 6, 2014
(together with Codicil (s) dated _____) and duly filed with the court.

2. The person (s) who would have a right to letters testamentary pursuant to Section 1412.1 is/are: [Enter "NONE" or specify name and interest]
DIANA PALMERI, by appointment in Will

3. Preliminary letters are requested for the following reasons:
Access to and liquidation of brokerage and bank accounts of deceased, sale of condominium owned by deceased, opening Estate checking account, filing and payment of Federal and NY State estate and income taxes.

4. Probate is expected to be completed by: unknown due to pending will contest proceeding

5. A contest [x] is   [ ] is not expected.

6. The testamentary assets of decedent's estate are estimated as follows: (describe and state value; annex a schedule if space is insufficient)

Personal Property: Cash in bank accounts, stocks and bonds in brokerage accounts, as described in Schedule A hereto.

Total Personal Property: $ 2,929,786

Real Property: Condominium apartment 20P at 372 Central Park West (estimated market value)

Total Real Property: $ 1,600,000

18 months rent, if applicable: _____

Total of 18 months rent: $ N/A

7. The liabilities of this estate are: Negligible

8. By provision in the propounded will, the applicant(s) [is/are]   [are not] required to file a bond or other security for the performance of his/her/their duties.

P-2 (10/95)

-1-

Your applicant (s) respectfully request the issuance to DIANA PALMER _____
_____
of preliminary letters testamentary upon qualifying.

Dated: June 6, 2016

Diana Palmer
Applicant

DIANA PALMER
Applicant

OATH & DESIGNATION OF PRELIMINARY EXECUTOR

STATE OF NEW YORK)
COUNTY OF —NEW YORK—) ss.:

I, the undersigned, DIANA PALMER _____ being duly sworn say:

1. **OATH OF PRELIMINARY EXECUTOR:** I am over eighteen (18) years of age and a citizen of the United States; I am an executor named in the Will described in the foregoing petition and will well, faithfully and honestly discharge the duties of preliminary executor and duly account for all money or property which may come into my hands. I am not ineligible to receive letters.

2. **DESIGNATION OF CLERK FOR SERVICE OF PROCESS:** I hereby designate the Clerk of the Surrogate's Court of New York _____ County, and his/her successor in office, as a person on whom service of any process issuing from such Surrogate's Court may be made, in like manner and with like effect as if I were served personally upon me whenever I cannot be found and served within the State of New York after due diligence used.

My domicile is: 750 Bridgewood Avenue, Oradel, New Jersey, 07649
(Street Address) (City/Town/Village) (State) (Zip)

Diana Palmer
(Signature of Petitioner)

DIANA PALMER
(Print Name)

On JUNE 6 _____ 20 16 , before me personally came

DIANA PALMER _____
to me known to be the person described in and who executed the foregoing instrument. Such person duly swore to such instrument before me and duly acknowledged that he/she executed the same.

EDWARD R. CURTIN
Notary Public, State of New York
No. 02CU0017740
Qualified in New York County
Commission Expires July 26, 20__

Notary Public
Commission Expires:
(Affix Notary Stamp or Seal)

Signature of Attorney: _____

Print Name: EDWARD R. CURTIN

Firm Name: Law Offices of Edward R. Curtin, Esq.   Tel No.: 212-686-4744

Address of Attorney: 220 West 71st Street, Suite 33, New York, NY 10023

NOTE: Each Preliminary Executor must complete a combined Oath & Designation of Preliminary Executor.

-2-

> OLGA PALMERI — 20
> DIANA PALMERI   40
> ANITA M GARZON 10
> VICTOR PALMERI 15
> CYNTHIA PALMERI 15/100

This is the **only** instrument that helps five Palmeris take over the 10 million dollars estate. They claimed that it was written by Sydney Fields, a ninety-six years old blind man. It did not have any witness, video, audio-tapes back up. It did not have any explanation and no testator's signature. Yet it was accepted by judge Mella under the monitor of our courts in the United States.

FIELDS, SIDNEY B - March, 2018

> MR. HAAS: The April 2016 report was disclosed during discovery; however, counsel did not submit the April 2016 report in opposition to the Motion for Summary Judgment. He decided for some reason now to submit it one day before oral argument. So, based on that, we have not had an opportunity to respond to the April 2016 report. We ask that your Honor reject the submission.
>
> THE COURT: Well, most definitely that is not part of the -- it's not part of the record in the Motion for Summary Judgment.
>
> So, did you want --
>
> MR. HAAS: Very good, Judge.
>
> MR. CHEN: May I just make one point on that, your Honor?
>
> THE COURT: I'm sorry. Mr. Messina, were you done?
>
> MR. MESSINA: I just have one other point to address on counsel's points. He referred to the deposition, sorry, the statement of the broker named Jeffrey Kern. That statement was not admittance to form. It's not a testimonial statement. It was not sworn to. Mr. Kern has not authenticated the statement. It was not submitted along with a business record certificate, and,

---

Margin note (sideways): This court paper recorded how the affidavit, on April 2016, was dismissed. It has the only sworn, made by the will drafter, explains why Sydney gave all his ten million dollars to those in-laws. Yet judge Milla still basing on a withdrawal sworn to release the money. The document also recorded how the only audio-tape in this case, provide by Vanguard's legal team, was attacked. It recorded Sydney's statements and they were totally ignored by the judge as well.

Palmerii dismissed most of the legal documents during the appeal process. Below is the related content they submitted to the courts.

sought to file objections to probate, but those objections were rejected by the Surrogate's Court and were never prosecuted. The Attorney General was served with the motion for summary judgment (a copy of the Notice of Motion is annexed hereto as **Exhibit K**) but did not participate in the motion. None of the exhibits submitted by the parties in connection with the motion for summary judgment included any of the rejected objections to probate by the Attorney General. (Exhibits H, I and J). These documents were not considered by the lower court.

23. The foregoing was but one example of documents that Appellant has improperly injected into the record for the first time on appeal. The following tables contain a list of documents, with page references, that are contained in the appendix that were never submitted to the court below. Some of the listed documents are not even reflected in the Appellant's Table of Contents (Exhibit E):

Page Number(s)	Document	Note
A-11-14 ①	Objection to Probate by the Attorney General of the State of New York dated June 3, 2016	These objections were rejected by the Surrogate's Court. The attorney general's office was served with the November 28, 2018 motion for summary judgment.
A-15-27 ②	Letter, Order and Decision concerning a proceeding for grandparent visitation in the New Jersey Superior Court.	

A-217-28 (3)	Transcript of purported conversation between Sydney Fields, Andrew Venne and Jeffrey Kern dated November 20, 2014	
A-229-237 (3)	Transcript of purported conversation between Sydney Fields and Jeffrey Kern dated March 26, 2015	
A-238-48 (3)	Transcript of purported conversation between Jeffrey Kern and Diana Palmeri dated April 22, 2015	
A-273, A-277, A-278, A-309-11, A-314-19, A-321-45, A-353-56, A-362, A-365-66, A-373, A-381-87. (These pages correspond to transcript pages 16, 47, 48, 87-89, 92-97, 99-123, 131-34, 140, 143-44, 151, 159-65)	Deposition transcript excerpts of Edward R. Curtin dated February 1, 2017 (4)	Excerpts of Mr. Curtin's transcript were submitted to the Surrogate's Court (Exhibit H, I and J), however Appellant submitted additional excerpts on appeal that were not submitted to the court below.
A-393, A-398 (These pages correspond to transcript pages 16 and 55)	Deposition transcript excerpts of Jill Curtin dated November 14, 2016 (4)	Excerpts of Ms. Curtin's transcript were submitted to the Surrogate's Court (Exhibit H and I), however Appellant submitted additional excerpts on appeal that were not submitted to the court below.
A-416-31 (These pages correspond to transcript pages 26-30, 94-102, 108-09)	Deposition transcript excerpts of Diana Palmeri dated November 15, 2016 (4)	Excerpts of Ms. Palmeri's transcript were submitted by Appellant to the Surrogate's Court (Exhibit I), however Appellant submitted additional excerpts on appeal that were not submitted to the court below.

A-129	Letter from Sydney Fields to Jeffrey Kern	
A-130-36	Affirmation of Edward R. Curtin, Esq. in support of issuance of preliminary letters testamentary dated June 17, 2016 with affidavit of service.	
A-158	Notice of Appearance of New York State Attorney General dated April 12, 2016	
A-183-85	Subpoena Duces Tecum on Dr. Janet Searle dated June 5, 2017	Doctor's record
A-191-92	Subpoena Ad Testificandum for Jeffrey A. Kern, dated February 21, 2017	
A-193, A-193B	Letter from Vanguard to Richard Alan Chen, Esq., dated March 17, 2017	
A-194	Letter from Richard Alan Chen, Esq. to Albert V. Messina Jr., Esq., dated March 24, 2017 (erroneously dated March 24, 2016)	Data from Vanguard
A-201-07	Transcript of purported conversation between Sydney Fields and Jeffrey Kern dated October 3, 2014	
A-208-216	Transcript of purported conversation between Sydney Fields, Anita and Jeffrey Kern dated November 7, 2014	

All provisions were listed in a page with a forgery initial. By substituting only one page they changed the whole will. It is easily to change the donations from 15% (of ten million dollars) to $500.

LAST WILL AND TESTAMENT OF
SYDNEY H. FIELDS

I, SYDNEY H. FIELDS, residing at 372 Central Park West, Apartment 20P in the City, County and State of New York, being of sound and disposing mind and memory, do make, publish and declare this to be my Last Will and Testament, hereby revoking all prior wills and codicils made by me.

FIRST: I order and direct the payment of all my just debts and testamentary expenses as soon as practicable after my death.

SECOND: I direct that all inheritance, estate and any other tax in respect of any inheritance under this my last will and testament by reason of any State, Federal or other laws new or hereafter in force (including any interest and penalties thereon) shall be paid by my executor or alternate executor out of my residuary estate as part of the expenses of administration thereof without apportionment.

THIRD: I give and bequeath $500 to the CITY COLLEGE FUND of the CITY UNIVERSITY OF NEW YORK, $500 to the UNITED JEWISH APPEAL OF NEW YORK, and $1,000 to the BARUCH COLLEGE FUND of the CITY UNIVERSITY OF NEW YORK.

FOURTH: All the rest, residue and remainder of my property and estate, both real and personal of every kind and description and wheresoever situated which shall belong to me or be subject to my disposal at the time of my death (my residuary estate) I give and bequeath as follows:

A. 20% (twenty percent) to OLGA PALMERI, currently residing at 80 Forest Avenue, Paramus, NJ 07652. If she should predecease me, I leave her share of my residuary estate to VICTOR PALMERI, Sr.
B. 35% (thirty-five percent) to DIANA PALMERI, currently residing at 750 Ridgewood Avenue, Oradel, NJ 07649. If she should predecease me, I leave her share in equal percentages to her husband, DAVID and each of their three children, with DAVID to act as Trustee of the shares left to their children until they reach majority.
C. 20% (twenty percent) to VICTOR PALMERI, Jr., currently residing at 80 Forest Avenue, Paramus NJ 07652. If he should predecease me, I leave his share to OLGA PALMERI.
D. 15% (fifteen percent) to CYNTHIA PALMERI, currently residing at 80 Forest Avenue, Paramus NJ 07652. If she should predecease me, I leave her share in equal shares to each of her children, per stirpes.
E. 10% (ten percent) to ANA MARIA GARZON YEPEZ, currently residing at Francisco Oliva Oe3-73 y Cap. Edmundo Chiriboga Casa #46, Quito, Ecuador, or her heirs if she should predecease me.

– 1 –

About this case

In 2016, we pursued a court case related to Sydney Fields' testament. My son's grandfather altered his will after his third wife died in 2015. At the time, he was 96 years old and blind. Without any video, audio tapes, and lacking valid witnesses, the will drafter Edward Curtin swore that Sydney intended to leave his $10 million estate to five in-laws of his deceased third wife. Compared to his two previous wills, the probated version reduced a $5 million donation to just $1,500 and left the Fields family with nothing.

This book reveals how a judge can recognize a sworn statement that was withdrawn during the court hearing. How she ignored the testator's statement recorded in Vanguard's phone system and let the probated "will" go within 45 minutes. Not just withdrew the affidavit, Curtin dismissed all his depositions later after that.

Over three years, we filed six appeals in three different courts, but we were rejected at every level. The U.S. Supreme Court requires that briefs and all supporting documents be presented in book format. When the case was ultimately dismissed, I decided to publish it as a book to expose how judges handle cases in American courtrooms. I concluded that our lawmakers tend to protect one another. They care more about their reputations than the integrity of our law.

This case discloses tragedies related to a Jewish family in the last one hundred years. Sydney Fields was born in 1918, one day after his father died from the Spanish Flu, a plague that killed 26 million people in the world. Doctor Philip risked his life to help Fishman's family. Watching the father's dead body being moved out of the room, he helped deliver a newborn son, Sydney. He signed both the death and birth certificates.

During the Great Depression, two of Sydney's uncles, who grew up with him as brothers, committed suicide because they couldn't find a job. Sydney survived adversity and refused to give up. He worked hard his entire life as the backbone of his family because he knew how sad children without a father felt. I believe that since God gave this family a hand back then, it is impossible that God would make things end up so ugly. Comparing with what the brave doctor did, it is a disgrace that the judge allowed Sydney's legacy to be stolen. I did not only protect Fields' assets; I also wish our world has more justice day by day, not less.

What happened during the process was extraordinary, and I felt as though we were being guided by a greater force that made everything happen coincidentally but predestined.

In 2015, I dated with guys on the internet. It happened that all the right persons left New York State suddenly or we were seriously sick when we were together. I had weird feelings and decided to step back. I even mentioned to my sister that Richard Fields might need my help. We had been divorced for a few years already and hardly saw each other during winter because we had nowhere to hang out in the cold weather. Before Christmas of 2015, I called him. If I waited until the weather turned warmer, that "will" would have passed through probate uncontested. The law requires that challenges must be made within one month.

Richard did need help. I realized many years later that he actually is autistic, which gave him good memory and high IQ as well. He once won the chess championship at New York City High School's tournament, and his college index is 4. If he'd received more affection from his parents, perhaps he would have a totally different life. Being autistic, he doesn't know how to deal with people. In some ways, he remained stuck in childhood, only expressing his own desires and oblivious to the feelings of others. Sadly, his unstable mother used him as a pawn in her conflicts with his father. He was bullied in school, which forced him to fight back violently. Because of that, he moved over ten times in his childhood, and that drove him crazy as well.

I divorced Richard in 1999. During a mental breakdown, he injured me by cutting my thumb and afterward received court-ordered psychiatric treatment. Despite everything, I still kept an eye on him even after the divorce. I bought him clothes, treated him to lunch, and took him to the barber.

We met in front of the library on a Saturday of 2016 New Year's Eve, right after I called him. Richard ran to me with a smile and said his father had died and without will probated. In a case like that, he deserves something by law. He said that if I helped him claim the estate, he would give half to me and our son, Lewis. That same night, I asked my brother-in-law, a lawyer, to draft a legal document to confirm Richard's promise.

I hardly see my sister, not more than three times a year. Coincidentally, as business partners, we had a rare dinner that we never had. We then went to a concert that we never cared to go to. Those activities gave me a chance to get the legal document on the second day.

The following day, Richard insisted on making a public notary for the document with his food stamp card and student ID. He ignored my opinion about waiting for a legal ID to come to do it. So just within three days, we had the agreement ready that encouraged me to start the court case when Richard collapsed.

On the fourth day, Edward Curtin appeared at Richard's adult home and announced Sydney's will. He said that the Fields family would receive nothing because Richard once threatened his father with some pictures. That was when he lost his mind, and I reminded him that psychiatric disorder can be forgiven by the law. Richard refused to answer my call because I said so.

Richard admitted that afterward, he had expected his father's money since he was three years old because his mother told him he deserved it. But he feared that if the court deemed him mentally unstable, an appointed guardian would send him to a mental hospital, and the inheritance would become meaningless. He warned that if we mentioned his mental condition, he would drop the case. His standards complicated everything during the legal fight.

Another coincidence is, after that dinner, four of my business partners did something I'd never done before. They escorted Richard to the subway and waited until he boarded. That made me do the same thing the next day when seeing him. On that platform, before one second of boarding, Richard answered my question and told me that our son Lewis's name was mentioned in his father's will. After that, he avoided me for nearly a month—that was the critical filing deadline for the court case. Still, the document and information he left were enough to motivate me to go forward. I took a day off for a lawyer's appointment. Richard didn't show up because he didn't like that I used his mental illness as a legal argument to fight back.

Without Richard's involvement, I must cancel the lawyer's appointment. There was another coincidence that my son Lewis had a day off by chance. He didn't want to pursue the case for he believed that 95% of wills are upheld. I convinced him that he had obligations to file a claim for his father's unpaid child support. I believed his grandfather Sydney should recognize his son's illness and leave something behind for his grandson. I was certain he loved Lewis deeply. Lewis agreed to be involved, and without his cooperation, I would've dropped the case entirely.

Besides that, I had a copy of Sydney's signature that looked different from the one on the probated will. It was from a check he sent at Lewis' first birthday. I'd lost countless items over the years, but somehow, I'd kept that one for 26 years. I felt like that was a sign to encourage me to proceed with the case.

A Chinese lawyer, Mr. Zhang, accepted our case because he had just helped a grandson secure part of an inheritance. But we were told in court that Lewis had no legal standing to contest the will unless his father was deceased. The judge gave us one week to get Richard's consent, without which we could not proceed. We recalled the situation—no lawyer would take our case except Zhang, who had not known such a rule. Without that misunderstanding, this case could not be filed in court and there would be no book.

We had only a week to convince Richard, but I couldn't reach him. The staff at the adult home thought I was harassing him and refused to pass along my calls. At my sister's urging, I spent two hours visiting Richard in person and didn't see him show up. He later claimed he came to the lobby after I left. Another coincidence at the same time—an American lawyer, brought in as co-counsel by Zhang, contacted Richard directly behind my back. Believing this lawyer worked for me, Richard signed a commitment with him. Without his unexpected interaction, we couldn't have moved forward with the case.

On the court day to file the case, I actually had another hearing for a rental business. My sister, who hardly helps me, insisted on meeting the tenant in court for me. That allowed me to see the American lawyer speaking privately with the will drafter Curtin in the hallway of the court building. It was suspicious that Mr. Zhang had to stay ten feet away from them. When returning to Zhang's law office, I was told that my $20,000 legal fee had been used up. Unless I provided another $20,000, I had no right to talk with them.

They actually did what lawyers never do—offered a contingency agreement for a testament. Even before the discovery phase, they hinted Richard would receive money, indicating a prearranged deal. It seemed they tried to get their legal fee by just convincing Richard, a mentally ill patient, to drop the case for a little bit of money. During the legal process, Palmarii never mentioned a settlement. What they offered must be a small amount that would disqualify Richard from SSI and lead to even more problems.

I reminded Richard about the situation he was in and meant to change lawyers. Richard rejected me, "Do you think you are smarter than lawyers?" Before he hung up the phone, I said to him, "All these years your mother got robbed by those lawyers who know more than us." At that moment, everything was out of control and fell apart.

The next morning, Lewis, who had never expressed concern for his father, asked me, "How's Richard?" That single question pushed me to try again. I called Richard, and this time, he simply answered me: "What do you want me to do? Come over to you?" We transferred the case successfully to a lawyer I had known for some time. He helped us receive the information we needed and we published everything we knew into this book.

It looked like all those coincidences were created by an invisible hand that helped us to continue. I don't believe this is the ending of our case since a long and painful journey has passed. Even though we lost forever, I have no regrets that $100,000 in legal fees was spent. It helped us to find out the truth: Sydney loved his family very much. His family fell apart because he refused to abandon a sick son, Richard. In the end, he lost the asset he accumulated all his life. Five nieces-in-law distributed $10 million from a 96-year-old blind man. The decision Judge Mella made shows us the dirty corners in America's courtrooms.

This book presents evidence to allow readers to decide whether perjury and forgery were involved in this case—whether a will was properly executed for a blind man when it was never read aloud to witnesses. Readers can determine if Sydney truly considered the Palmariis as his family when he had barely seen them in decades. This book reminds us how easily crimes can be committed through sworn statements, misleading affidavits, and backroom deals, then dismissed as if nothing happened.

Appeals were ignored, but that doesn't mean that things are done. Since July 2020, we have complained to the NYS Commission on Judicial Conduct and still wait for their decision. I will turn this case into a book, then into a script. Let it become an ongoing story, waiting for a response from a so-called democracy system.

Being mistreated, I can't stop worrying about the government's debt. In this book, I submitted proposals to solve the problem. When you are concerned with big disasters in this world, private loss becomes insignificant automatically.

Related Book Reviews

Reader K said this is very thought provoking: *Being part of the fraternity and practicing law for the past twenty years, I was quite surprised that I had never across this book or case earlier in my career of professional academia in any form.*

Dee De
The actual court proceeding and judgments were quite enriching and made the content stronger overall. You can just breeze through it to enjoy the book its imperative that you take your time and absorb all the details.

Jambalia
A courtroom drama that is bound to enthrall you. Do not get discouraged by the actual case proceedings and summaries in judicial format. It is quite interesting to go over the jargon used. An informative experience.

Rey Rey
Someone who has never been to court I had no idea the complex nature of what goes on in the court room. Very good read and really like it.

Reader Today
Drama that is nice and get to see actual cases and how they go. Recommend to others who want to see what court proceeding look like.

Kimiko Sanford
What utterly disgusted and baffled me was the court's approach towards the matter and how one family's appeals were constantly ignored without due analysis in the series of events. Definitely a must read for all the law makers.

Caitlin Webster
The author's attention to presenting the events of the court case as exactly as possible astounds me since it demonstrates the weaknesses of the justice system as it is manipulated in favor of prominent individuals…

Immanuel Chen
The proceeding of the court cases was something that is sadly a common occurrence, the author did well to highlight the underhanded tactics some people use to make the events of the case go their way from forged signatures and denial of mental conditions.

Roberto Loftin
It was sad to read that. If things continue as they are, this wonderful country could collapse from its economic debts within a few decades, but all hope is not lost because the author offer some viable measures to lower the debt and further strengthen the economy.

Magdalena Choi
The story of how a family fell apart completely with members going through the madness of greedy was disheartening one, but such is the case of some court cases around the country. At the very least the author showed the grim nature of such cases.

Ignacio Clark
It was an interesting read, because it shared with the readers the different lingos used in a judicial case. Aside from the information, it also offers a terrible situation that will make reader feel sorry for the family.

Theresa Hopper
The plot of Field's series of real-life courtroom events felt like a detective mystery off and on while going through the multiple wills and changes that were made to them over a period of time. Slow moving but interesting.

Jamison Everett
As a person with a mental condition myself, I can relate to how hard it is to make a person believe you or trust your words. The events that transpire in this book are an excellent yet grim display of injustice even amongst family.

Norah Larsen
I wasn't anticipating a short course on the economics share between two of the most influential nations in the world, the United States and China, but the book was engrossing to read.

Carl M.
Hard subject to tackle but Field's does a good job putting her family case forward to seek help and unveil the ugly and unfair side of the American judicial system. It was like an emotional roller coaster for me.

Janelle York
The majority of this book's material can be regarded as guidance on how to improve the state of the country, as recommendations for improving people's welfare and social security, to mention a few examples are shown.

Henrietta Murray
Strong and thought-provoking brief by Pia Fields. It is jaw dropping and rather pathetic how much she had to spend in terms of legal fees in order to defend her husband and what was theirs' to begin with and yet the debt manages to multiply.

Roderick Shaw
The twist and turns of the case, arguments and facts makes this book very interesting. If it wasn't for the proper court orders and writings in the text, this could make quite an intense family saga.

Nataly Montes
I was engrossed over the section that discussed the relationship between the US and the Chinese government, as it was unbiased and instead offers a means to solve the ongoing disputes with less hostility and instead of a more understanding mindset.

Tierra Neel
Reading this book was an emotional experience, as the story of how a family fell apart completely with members going through madness in their solitude reminded me of how even in court, justice can't always prevail.

Raven Potter
The author attempts to explain away the necessity of changing the mindset of the people on viewing money as the ultimate goal in life, and instead cherish the moments we have with friends and family.

Janiya Spencer
With impressive attention to detail and the sharing of more specific facts, the book was a treasure trove of information as it allows reader to grasp the complexities of the court case.

Marjorie Martin
Brilliant way to seek help and bring the unjust court proceedings into the limelight. I have decided to use this as a case study for my Law course students in the coming semester.

I appreciate the above book review writers. They make me feel that someone did catch my meaning, and I am not alone.

Supreme Court of the United States
Office of the Clerk
Washington, DC 20543-0001

Scott S. Harris
Clerk of the Court
(202) 479-3011

January 27, 2020

Mr. Richard J. Fields
2830 Pitkin Avenue
Brooklyn, NY 11208

    Re: In Re Richard J. Fields
        No. 19-410

Dear Mr. Fields:

The Court today entered the following order in the above-entitled case:

The petition for rehearing is denied.

Sincerely,

Scott S. Harris, Clerk

NO. 19-_____

In the
Supreme Court of the United States

RICHARD J. FIELDS,

Petitioner,

V.

DIANA PALMERI, OLGA PALMERI, VICTOR PALMERI,
CYNTHIA PALMERI and ANA GARZON YEPEZ,

Respondents.

On Petition for an EXTRAORDINARY Writ of
Mandamus **to the New York Court of Appeals**

PETITION FOR
EXTRAORDINARY WRIT OF CERTIORARI OF
MANDAMUS

RICHARD J. FIELDS
PETITIONER PRO SE
2830 PITKIN AVENUE
BROOKLYN, NY 11208
(718) 235-0900

AUGUST 16, 2019

SUPREME COURT PRESS ♦ (888) 958-5705 ♦ BOSTON, MASSACHUSETTS

QUESTIONS PRESENTED

This case relates to a 9 million dollar estate of a 96 year old blind man and his family which had three mental patients. Within one hour Judge Rita Mella in the New York County Surrogate's Court gave all Sydney Fields' estate to the nieces of his third wife (she predeceased him). After that all the appellate courts rejected my appeal. That is why I am here looking for justice. Below are questions raised in my case. Thank you for your attention.

- Should we ignore a <u>forged initial because our law does not require an initial to make a Will</u> valid? How about people falsifying a will by switching its pages?
- Should we allow lawyers to <u>conceal a person's psychiatric problem before</u> accusing him and causing him a big loss? (Nine Million Dollars)
- Should we allow a judge to <u>recognize a will- drafter's affirmations rather than the decedents' statements</u> which were recorded on audiotape?
- Shouldn't video and audiotapes be mandatory and required by law for Will drafters who provide service for <u>blind people</u>? Shouldn't we at least require their Wills being read aloud in front of the witnesses?

LIST OF THE PARTIES

Petitioner

- Richard J. Fields (Pro Se)

Respondents

- Diana Palmeri
- Olga Palmeri
- Victor Palmeri
- Cynthia Palmeri
- Ana Garzon Yepez

Name of Party to Whom Writ of Mandamus is Sought

- New York Court of appeals

PETITION FOR A WRIT OF MANDAMUS

Surrogate's Court of New York County Judge Rita Mella on the date 26th March 2018 dismissed my objection to the probating of Sydney's Will of 2014. (App.12a-19a). Her decision has been published already.

On the date of 25th Sep, 2018 the First Judicial Department in the Country of New York denied my appeal of an order of the Surrogate's Court of New York County and on the date of 27th Dec, 2018 they denied my motion to reopen my appeal (case number # M-3860/M-4067). A copy of that decision appears in the Appendix. (App.4a-5a).Decision not being published yet.

On the date of 31st Jan, 2019 the supreme Court of the State of New York and New York County dismissed our case (#101305/2018) and told me to appeal it to the Appellate Division. (App.3a) Decision not being published.

On the date of 2nd April, 2019 the State of New York Court of Appeals denied my appeal MO no. 2019-125 and admitted that their order does not finally determine the proceeding within the meaning of the constitution. (App.1a-2a)

On the date of 27th June, 2019 the State of New York Court of Appeals Denied my motion for re-argument (App. 20a).

Decision are being published already.

OPINIONS BELOW

The order of the Court of appeals for the State of New York, dated April 2, 2019 in included below at App.1a. The Order of the New York Appellate Division, First Judicial Department date, December 27, 2018 is included below at App 15a The underlying opinion of the Surrogate's Court of New York County Judge Rita Mella on the date 26th March, 2016 is include below at App 1a-8a.That court's Decree of Probate, dated July 20, 2018 is included below at App 8a,

---

The New York Court of Appeals denied a timely motion for re-argument on June 27, 2019. (App.20a) This petition for Extraordinary Writ of Mandamus is filed pursuant to Sup.Ct.R.20.4 (a). This Court has Jurisdiction under 28.U.S.C 1651

- due to the long procedural history in this case, the New York Court of Appeals notes that it is order of April 2, 2019 pertains to the December 27, 2018 Appellate Division order (App 15a), and not to the earlier order of September 25, 2018.

RULE 20 STATEMENT

- Name and Function of Parties to Whom Mandamus is Sought to be Directed

Petitioner seeks a writ of mandamus issued to the New York Court of Appeals.

- Specific Relief Sought

The New York Court of Appeals dismissed the Petitioner's appeal on the grounds that "Such (appellate) order does not finally determine the proceeding within the meaning of constitution; and it is further Petitioner seeks and order directed New York Court of Appeals"

This case involves the probate of the will of the late Sydney H. Fields, father of the Petioner Richard Fields. The Decree of Probate (App 8a) has been issued excluding the Petitioner who is the child of the decedent. Nothing can have more finality than such a judgment and the transfer of assets away from his son and rightful heir, the Petitioner is imminent without the intervention of this Court.

The Petitioner seeks the issuance of a Writ of Mandamus to the New York court of Appeals with directions that a final judgment is in place and the appeal of the Petitioner is ripe for review. The Petitioner further requests review by this court of the history, documents, and testimony in this case which should conclusively determine that the Petitioner is a rightful heir; and igitur direct the New York County Surrogate's Court to vacate the Order of Probate and enter judgment in favor of Petitioner.

- Why Petitioners Have Filed for Relief in This Court
  Petitioner timely filed appeals in the New York Appellate Division And the New York Court of Appeals. Instead of addressing the issues On the merits, the Court of Appeals "punted" by fallaciously claiming that it was premature to file and appeal claiming that the lower court orders were not finally determinative.
  Thus with remedies in the New York State courts now exhausted, the Petitioner turns to the United States Supreme Court for a Writ of Mandamus.

STATEMENT OF THE CASE

On March 26, 2018, Surrogate's Court fo New York County Judge Rita Mella dismissed my objection to the probating of Sydney's Will of 2014(App 12a-19a) Her decision has been published already.

On September 25, 2018 the first Judicial Department in the Country of New York denied my appeal of an order of the Surrogate's Court of New York County and on the date of December 27, 2018 they denied my motion to reopen my appeal (case number #M-3860/M-4067). A copy of that decision appears in Appendix (App 4a-5a)

On January 31, 2019 the Supreme Court of the State of New York and New York County dismissed my case (#101305/2018) and told me to appeal it to the Appellate Division.(App 3a)

On April 2, 2019 the State of New York Court of Appeals denied my appeal MO no. 2019-125 (App.1a-2a) and on the grounds that the order of the appellate Division did not finally determine the proceeding within the meaning of the Constitution. The Court of Appeals did not explain or elaborate on what constitutional standard it was relying upon in its order.

On the date of June 27, 20a9 the State of New York court of Appeals denied my motion for re-argument (App. 20a)

REASONS FOR GRANTING THE WRIT

My name is Richard Fields. I am receiving psychiatric treatment (App168a, 169a) and living on the SSI program for more than twenty years. Because of my psychotic behavior Fields family members did not contact each other all these years. Taking advantage of the situation, four nieces of Sydney Fields' third wife (she predeceased him) distribute my father's 9 million dollar estate. Compared with the previous will the 2014 will increased the Palmeris' shares from 1% to 100%, double of what Sydney gave to his wife, their aunt. The 2014 will also reduce the charity's share from 4 million dollars to $1,500 without any explanation from the decedent. For that reason the attorney general of NY State considered that a felony was involved. (App 21a-24a)

Below is what actually happened:

- **THEY COMMITTED PERJURY ABOUT SYDNEY'S VISION**

Five days before the Will was signed the 96 years old testator, Sydney Fields, talked to the broker from Vanguard: "I can't read, I can't read, I can't read any type, you know, and, and that's why I can't handle those pages., I, I, I, I, I, can't, I can't read them, no, I can't read. . . . .I mean, with my magnifying glass I can read large print, but I can't read anything that's— that's on papers." His statement was recorded by Vanguard's phone system. (App 56a)

Eye exam report provided by Janet Serle confirmed Sydney's vision as below: On Dec 5th 2014, blind in both eyes.(App 43a line2-4) On Sep 3rd 2014, legally blind:(App 44a line 2-4) right eye was totally blind and his left eye could not count fingers from 3 feet away (App 42a chart). The 2014 will was signed on Oct 6th 2014, between legal blind to blind. The respondent's lawyers ordered and forwarded those records to me in 2016 but tried to dismiss them in 2018.

However, the judge believed that Sydney could read just because a magnifying glass is mentioned. "Here the fact that the attesting witnesses could not confirm whether decedent had his magnifying glass that day (the attorney-drafter and one of the witnesses testified that he had.)App16a line 4-8. Below was the witness, wife of will-drafter Edward Curtin, Jill Curtin said:

"I have a memory of a magnifying glass. It's a black rectangle with a handle, but I am not sure if that was Mr. Fields. I believe he might have, you know . . . ." (App 76a) That Will was signed in Curtin's small apartment and who else was there and needed a magnifying glass that day? When again Jill Curtin answered the question about: "Did you see Mr. Fields read with or without the magnifying glass?" She refused to confirm and said: "I have this little memory of him with the magnifying glass, but . . . " (App 77a)

Edward Curtin showed the same contradictions in his deposition. "He was there with a magnifying glass. We looked at every page. Whether he—I wasn't inside his mind to know whether he actually read every single word." (App 79a) He meanwhile confirmed that: "I think there was a combination of that. We sat side by side on the final version of the will and in part he was using his magnifying glass to read sections and part I would read to him. I think he also used his magnifying glass to ascertain that what I was saying was there, was there."(App 78a last paragraph)

Respondent Diana Palmeri said: "Yes, I observed him reading . . . . He used the magnifying glass." (App 66a)

Their lawyer Haas said: "The fact that the decedent had a limited—this is limited eyesight, again, judge, is a nonissue. All right? There is nothing to prevent a person who has limited eyesight from signing a will. Nothing provided as to the fact that he couldn't read or he couldn't see and simply said legally blind is a "far cry from being actually blind. An actually blind person may still execute a will . . . . (App 26a)

Their other lawyer Messina told the Judge: "Sidney Fields actually states that he can read with a magnifying glass. "In addition to the fact that the statement may say legally blind, which is a far cry from being actually blind. An actually blind person may still execute a will . . . ." (App 27a)

Under their intensive convincing Judge Mella also concluded: "The fact that decedent had some visual impairment, even to the point of 'legal' blindness as objectant argues, does not change this conclusion because blind persons may make wills. (App 16a 2nd Para)

- **THEY DID NOT READ THE WILL OUT LOUD TO A BLIND MAN**

Judge Mella ignored one thing: For a blind man the law requires the Will drafter to read the will out loud in front of the witnesses (*Matter of Hubert*, 26 Misc. 461 57 N.Y. Supp. 648 *Affd.*, 48 App Div. 91, 62

N.Y. Supp. 932, 98 quoted in Annotated Consolidated Laws of New York 1917. Also See Matter of *MacCready*, 82 Misc. 2d 531, 369 N.Y.S.2d 325 (1975). <u>In this case, even Edward Curtin himself as well as the witnesses admitted that there was never a Will read out loud in the process. When Curtin explained the Will side by side there were no witnesses present as well.</u>

Below are Edward and Jill Curtin who answered the question about if they read the will out loud:

Q: Did you hear Mr. Curtin read the will to Mr. Fields?
A: No. I don't know—I did not know what was in the will.
Q: Did Mr. Curtin read the Will to Sydney Fields out loud?

A: Not in my presence. (App 76a-line 14-21)
Question to Edward Curtin:

Q: You say in your affirmation: Prior to signing his will I read the entire text thereof to Mr. Fields and he concurred with it accurately as reflected in his testamentary wishes?

A: That's right.

Q: When did that happen?

A: Prior to the time we did the actual—we called the witnesses in to do the execution.

Q: So the witnesses were not there when this took place, is that correct?

A: That is correct. (App 79a-80a)

Q: Is it correct to state that the witnesses never heard you read off to Mr. Fields the fourth paragraph of the will on page 1 concerning the beneficiaries as to what their percentages would be, et cetera?

A: The witnesses did not hear me read any of the provision of the will at any time. (App 85a-86a)

It is obvious that in this case no witness could tell if Mr. Fields knew his will before signing it.

- **THEY USED A FORGER INITIAL TO SWITCH A PAGE AND FALSIFY A WILL**

In the 2014 will all distributions were listed on the first page. Switching that page can falsify the whole will. My handwriting expert Mr. Curt Baggett confirmed that the initial on that page was forged. (App 109a, 113a) The circle on the bottom of the forged S was much large then the S that Sydney signed. It was handled perfectly without a mark X which Sydney always required when he signed. It is obvious that the initial was made carefully by someone who could see. Disqualify Mr. Baggett helping them go nowhere.

Since no witness knew whether the 2014 will was the same will that Mr. Fields signed the distributions could easily have been changed by switching the page. Our argument is: when switching one page can gave them the distribution they need why should they bother to forge the signature in the last page, committed undue influence or duress? To answer our argument they simply announced: American law does not require initials to make a will valid. The judge repeated what they said.

Judge Mella agreed their opinion and said:

"Even if the court were to consider this letter an affidavit of an expert, there is no requirement that a testator initial the pages of a will for it to be valid. Instead, all that is required in this regard is that it have been signed "at the end thereof (id). The opinion letter is not addressed to the real issue-whether it is decedent's signature at the end of the will—a fact that objectant does not contest with competent evidence" (App 17a last paragraph)

Judge Mella also believed forged one initial was insignificant. She ignored us because we did not challenge initials in the other pages and signature in the last page.

THEIR DISPOSITIVE TERMS OF A PROPOSED INSTRUMENT WAS BASED ON CURTIN'S AFFIRMATION

When saying a blind man can make a will the judge also mentioned: "Here, the attorney-drafter testified that the dispositive terms of a proposed instrument were provided to him by decedent himself and confirmed those dispositive provisions of the will orally to decedent shortly before execution" (App 16a line 17- line22)

Instrument that was recognized by Judge Mella had only names and numbers. It had no date, no signature, no stamp, and most of all did not mention anything about altering the ill. That instrument was written with strong strokes, in a straight line, and in an identical way. It does not look like it was written by a 96 year old blind man who can hardly control his pen but looks like it was made by cutting and pasting on a computer. (App 122a-123a)

Curtin told us what happened when he received the instrument:

> Q: Did Mr. Fields make out this sheet in front of you?
> A: No.
> Q: Can you tell me what he said and what you said, concerning when this was handed to you?
> A: He said this is the way I want to have the— his estate, his residuary estate distributed.
> Q: And, do you know if this document was made out by Mr. Fields?
> A: I don't know for certain, but he is the only person that gave it to me.

In this picture, the distributions of a 9 million dollars will were based on an instrument. However, as the only back-up materials the instrument itself needed Curtin's affirmations to back it up. Curtin told us it was only Sydney who gave him the instrument orally; the numbers 20, 40, 15, and 10 mean the distribution of Sydney's residuary estate. (App 87a)

He also has to explain why there was a 5% difference between the instrument and the will. Curtin said Sydney told him on the phone to switch 5% from Diana to Victor. (App 83a)

On whole, the names and numbers on that instrument had nothing to do with the Will. It became the dispositive provisions of the will just because Curtin attesting to it.

A draft of the 2006 will has only Curtin's markup was present as the back-up document for the 2016 will as well. Curtin wrote down whatever without any audiotapes recording his conversation with Sydney. (App 124a-128a)

- **THEY COMMITTED PERJURY ABOUT THE RELATION SHIP BETWEEN SYDNEY AND THE PALMERIS**

  - The 2006 Will Shows Sydney Worried Some- one May Contest His Will

    Another perjury Curtin made was he mentioned the relationship between Sydney and the Palmeris. He attested: *"In the previous superseded will, Mr. Fields had left the bulk of his estate to his wife, Teresa Fields, but when she died in September of 2014, Mr. Fields was compelled to have a new will drafted, wherein he provided for his residuary estate to be distributed amongst members of his deceased wife's family whom he had come to embraces as his own family."* In the deposition he admitted that "Those are my words" (App 81a)

    Without requesting any back-up material Judge Mella accept Curtin's perjuries and said *"that is a natural will benefiting members of the family of decedent's spouse, with whom decedent was close and whom he considered his family."* (App 14a last para)

    However, in the 2006 will Sydney seriously put down a statement which reflected that he noticed and tried to prevent someone stealing his money. He said:

    "If any beneficiary other than my wife Teresa Fields shall in any manner directly or indirectly attempt to contest or oppose the validity of this will or commence, maintain or join in except as a party defend- ant, or be in any way, directly or indirectly, interfere or instrumental in the institution or maintenance of any action or proceeding in any court for the purpose of preventing the probate of this will or for the purpose of attacking the validity of this will or any provisions thereof, then in such event such beneficiary shall forfeit his or her share hereunder . . . ., (App 144a) That statement was written as the TENTH in the 2006 Will. (App 142a)

As the will drafter Curtin's used "the bulk of his estate" instead of 50% to mention what Teresa had in the 2006 Will and then made it to 100% in the 2014 will.

The 2006 will only allowed Teresa left the money to Victor but nobody else. In the 2014 Will Curtin said Sydney distributed his assets to 5 Palmeris but without any reference. That obvious was a perjury comparing with what Sydney wrote down.

<u>Information from Vanguard's phone records proves their relationship was not as good as Curtin claims.</u>

Five days before signing the Will Sydney tried to arrange a huge fund transfer without letting Diana and Curtin know. He could not read documents but refused to get help from Diana and he was very afraid to let Edward Curtin know about his assets as well. He made the broker travel from Philadelphia to help him finish the transfer. Diana knew that 1.5 years later when Sydney died.

After the 2014 will was signed and a half year before Sydney died he got an exemption from the bank and limited Diana's POA to only one account and explained his worries (App 60a)

> Mr. Kern: So at Vanguard when we add an agent, it's done at the account level, not at the fund level. So if you name an agent it would be for all the funds in that account?
>
> Mr. Fields: Well, well, I mean, that puts me at a disadvantage, I mean, she had, she has access to all of my accounts and I could be dispossessed if I have an argument with her or anything. I wanted to limit her to one account, is there any way that can be done?
>
> Mr. Kern: Uh,
>
> Mr. Fields: I mean, can I open up a, a, can I shift that account to, to another title? (App 61a)

The above conversation shows Sydney did not intend to give all his assets to the Palmeris like what the 2016 will said. He kept the money from her because he has another arrangement. (App 64a)

Until he died, as the executor, Sydney did not release money to the Palmeri family according to what Teresa Fields' Will said.

Diana's deposition also shows that the Palmeris' relationship with Sydney was not close enough to make them have all Sydney's assets. Sydney never met Ana Garzon Yepez before 2014 his wife died. Victor Palmeri Jr. lived in Hawaii and Diana was only sure Sydney met Victor he was in high school. Cynthia Palmeri lived in NC and came to NJ twice per years. Diana moved back to NJ from the West Coast after the year of 2000, Sydney went to NJ with his wife only, on holidays, a few times a year. He never took a trip with them and never spent overnight in their home. (App 69a-72a)

On the whole only Curtin's affirmation is not enough to explain this perplexing question: How did distant stranger relations inherit double of what their aunt Teresa Fields would have received. The most obvious explanation is fraud, unless have strong evidences and they have none.

- **THEY DON'T HAVE A VALID WITNESS AND THE WILL HAS MAJOR MISTAKES**

- **Suzanne Lehman Refused to Confirm Basic Things**

    Q. Did that happen? Did Mr. Fields say, yes that's my will and that is why you signed the affidavit?
    - To tell you the truth, the process was never—I mean, Mr. Fields spoke and agreed.

    . . . Whether he spoke up, I don't remember that he did and he said it to me. But it was definitely being led by his lawyer. (App 73a)

    Suzanne Lehman refused to say she saw Mr. Fields sign the Will as well. Sitting here today do you recall watching him sign? Answer: I do not recall. (App 74a).

Judge ignored the fact and said "when there is a contemporaneous affidavit of the attesting witnesses reciting the facts of due execution a presumption of proper execution arises" (App 16 a first para)

- **Will Pages That Witnesses Signed Had Serious Mistakes**

In the 2014 Will Curtin mention Testator is "her" instead of "his". It said "On this 6th day of October, 2014, Sydney H. Fields, the above-named testator, in our presence subscribed and sealed the foregoing instrument and declared the same to be her Last Will and Testament: and we, thereupon, at <u>her</u> request and in <u>her</u> presence and in the presence of each other, have hereunto subscribed our names as attesting witnesses." (APP 143a last paragraph) This is a clear evident that the attesting witnesses saw a woman but not a man signing the will.

Another issue was in the witnesses' affidavit that made the document invalid as well. That affidavit date was typed on July 26th, 2006 and was altered on Oct 6th, 2014 by pen. According to the Notary Public law, a notarized document must be only typed or hand written. It will be invalid when it was composed by both way. (App 155a) They even did not provide witness' affidavit when probated the Will until we question about it. The above mistakes are enough to disqualify the 2014 Will yet Mella believed: "Objectant failed to present any evidence of a mistake."

- **Regarding the Wills**

- **The Will of 1997 (App 130a-136a)**

In 1997 May 20th Sydney Fields made his first will. That was about two years after he received my harassing pictures, and filed an order of protection. It was also after he lost the right to visit Kenneth's children because he refused to listen to Kenneth to end the relationship with me.

In that Will he gave Victor $65,000; gave each children of Cynthia Palmeri and Diana Palmeri Lukac $5,000; gave his Uncle Solomon Rosen $35,000; gave Richard J. Fields $35,000; and he said: For reasons best known to my son Kenneth L Fields, I deliberately make no provision for him in this will and it is my intention that he received no part of my estate.

Upon the death of Teresa Fields, ... the net of all my estate and income shall be distributed by the Trustees as follows:

> 25% to the City College, 10% to the United Jewish Appeal of New York.

> 25% to my granddaughter Elizabeth Fields 25% to my grandson Alex Fields.

> 15% to my grandson Lewis D. Fields. He also designated Pia Fields as Lewis Fields' trustee.

Again having me arrested in 1994-1996, in his 1997 Will Sydney Fields still considered I am his son because he noticed that I was sick. Instead he left nothing to Kenneth who forced my father to end the relationship with me.

- **The Will of 2006 (App 134a-143a)**

It looks like Sydney was being undue influenced when set up the 2006 will. Teresa wanted to actually control and arrange money she inherited from Sydney instead of giving it back to Fields' family and charity eventually as the 1997 will indicated. Vision getting worse day by day, Sydney was in a duress environment and had no choice. For keeping the donation he put his family members away and had to list some reasons. He noticed that someone behind Teresa wanted to have his money and he strongly against them. In the 2006 will he only allowed the 50% that Teresa inherited from him forward to Victor. On the will of 2006, Sydney again gave nothing to Olga, Cynthia Palmeri and Diana Palmeri (only gave $5,000 to each of their children) To Victor Palmeri, Jr, Lewis D, Fields and his uncle Solomon Rosen he gave the equal amount $35,000. He made no provision for his sons Kenneth, Richard and his grandchildren Elizabeth and Alex.

He kept the charity amount: 25% to the City College Fund of the City University of NY; 10% to the United Jewish Appeal of NY; 15% to the Baruch College Fund of the City University of NY.

He did allow 50% left to Victor Palmeri Jr after Teresa died. But again that was only when Teresa live longer than him and beside that he prevented anyone else took his money

3, The 2014 Will (App 154a-163a)

The distributions of the 2014 will only gave $500 to the CITY COLLEGE FUN, $500 to JEWISH APPEAL OF NEW YORK, and $1,000 to the BARUCH COLLEGE instead of 4.5 million dollars in the previ- ous will.

All the rest, residue and remainder of Sydney's property and estate is distributed as below:
- 20% to Olga Palmeri., if she should prede- cease me, I leave her share of my residuary estate to Victor Palmeri, Sr.
- 35% to Diana Palmeri. If she should prede- cease me, I leave her share in equal percen- tages to her husband, DAVID and each of their three children, with DAVID to act as trustee of the shares left to their children until they reach majority.
- 20% to Victor Palmeri, Jr. If he should prede- cease me, I leave his share to Olga Palmeri.

- 15% to Cynthia Palmeri, if she should prede- cease me, I leave her share in equal shares to each of her children, per stirpes.
- 10% to Ana Maria Garzon Yepez, currently residing at Francisco Oliva Oe3-73 y Cap Edmundo Chiriboga Casa #46 Quito, Ecuador, or her heirs if she should predecease me.

• My arguments are raised as below:

- Sydney never mentioned Olga Palmeri, her sister in-law, in his previous two wills. However she became the number one beneficiary in the 2014 will. It looks like it was Olga's children made the will and endorsed their mother.
- In his previous wills Sydney never worried how the money would go if his beneficiaries predeceased him. The 2014 will reflected the beneficiaries' worries and seriously protected each of their families' benefit. It looks like the will was made by beneficiaries themselves rather than Sydney.
- The 2014 will give Victor 20% and allowed him to inherited 20% when his mother died. It comforted the mother and satisfied the son. Victor would have 50% of the estate if Teresa lived longer than Sydney. He therefor cannot stand Diana got more than him. The 5% transfer back and ford reflected fighting in palmeri's family. Curtin committed perjury when he answered how Sydney indicated him to make the change. He said "there may have been a phone conversation, I don't recall " (App 83a)
- That dispositive instrument they presented had only names and numbers (App 122a) However, in the 2014 will it list Ana Maria Garzon Yepez lived in Francisco Oliva Oe3-73 y Cap Edmundo Chiriboga Casa #46 Quito, Ecuador. How did Sydney know and remember that long address and forward it accurately to Curtin? Yet judge Mella believed "The testimony of the attorney-drafter, which estab- lished that the beneficiaries had no direct involve- ment in the

preparation of the execution of the will (App 14a to 15a) She believed so because Curtin's affirmations said so.

- **Credibility of Edward Curtin and Their Counsels Are Questionable**

　　Regarding this case the NYS Attorney General's objection not only attacked the Palmeri family they also believed "other persons acting independently or in concert or in private with Diana". (App 22a) Curtin is a retired lawyer living in a rental apartment which he uses it as an office. Sydney knew him from an advertisement in the street many years ago. Sydney never had business contacts with him except to let him draft wills. Our discoveries prove that the assumptions of the NYS Attorney General are correct. Curtin's credibility is questionable.

　　1. Vanguard's phone records show Sydney did not trust Edward Curtin at all. When broker Kern suggested him to get Curtin to fill out forms for the fund transfers Sydney was very panicky.

　　Mr. Kern: And a question came up, so you mentioned that you have a meeting with your attorney this afternoon?

　　Mr. Fields: Yes.

　　Mr. Kern: Do you believe that your attorney would be able to help you out with these forms?

　　Mr. Fields: No, no, he knows nothing about the forms.

　　Mr. Kern: Okay.

　　Mr. Fields: I am not discussing any forms with him.

Mr. Kern: Okay, okay, that was just a question that had come up if the attorney could, could assist you with this.

Mr. Fields: No, no. No, I'm no, no, he has—he doesn't know anything about these forms, so I didn't mention anything to him. (App 59a)

- **THEY DISMISSED THE RECORD WHEN IT WAS MADE UP OF AFFIRMATIONS**

Curtin did not mention Sydney's vision problem in the affirmation he made in April, 2016. All he said was "As the supervisor who drafted the Will and supervised the execution thereof, I attest and affirm without qualification that Sydney Fields was completely competent, lucid and keenly aware of the contents of the Will and the dispositions made therein." They tried to dismiss that affirmation in 2018.

Large portion of the document that we exchanged during the discovery period were dismissed by the respondent's counsel in their motion to the First Judicial Department of the County of New York. That include:

Eye doctor Janet Searle confirmed that Sydney was blind in both eyes. They denied it even though they are the one who ordered it and forwarded us.

Sydney's autograph and his lawsuit that proof how much Sydney loved his family. They dismiss it because it put Palmeris in embarrass position.

Affidavit Edward Curtin made in April, 2016 from there Sydney's vision problem was not mentioned at all. They dismiss it because we basing on that questioning Curtin's credibility.

They dismissed most of the depositions even though they quoted the same thing as we quoted. Their excuse is that those documents were not filed in the Surrogate's Court. We spent $100,000 to depose witnesses and make the discoveries from 2014 to 2016. Since Judge Mella dismissed us within 60 minutes we had no chance and no need to file those documents in the Surrogate's Court any more. They used that as excuse to stop us from using those documents when we filed an appeal in the Appellate Court.

They dismissed all the transcripts of the USB provided by Vanguard. They cannot deny that Sydney's voice was recorded in it and they challenged the submitting process. In the court hearing their lawyer Messina asked the judge to ignore the flashdrive and said: I just have one other point to address on counsels appoints. He referred to the statement of the broker named Jeffrey Kern. That statement was not admittance to form. It's not a testimonial statement. It was not sworn to. Mr. Kern has not authenticated the statement. It was not submitted along with a business record certificate." (App 27a line 11- 19).

Their reason include:

Vanguard is "an out-of-state party". They meanwhile forwarded us Sydney's account information provided by such an out-of-state party.

The flashdrive "was not accompanied by a business record certification." The flashdrive was provided by Vanguard's legal department and attached with a letter signed by their legal aide. They said that was a flashdrive without a certification.

"Kern was not "sworn to". The flashdrive recorded conversations between Jeffrey Kern and Sydney. Vanguard provided it to us without Kern's comments or opinions and that is why it is not sworn to.

"The USB contains alleged unauthenticated recordings". They received the flashdrive six months before the court hearing. They did nothing and simply dismiss the transcript my lawyer forwarded to them.

During the appeal, they avoided answering my arguments but used strategies to dismiss my motions. The clerk in the Surrogate's Court helped us to appeal our case Pro Se to the New York State Supreme Court Appellate Division. The respondent's lawyer rejected my appeal motion with the reason that I was supposed to have Mr. Chen as my lawyer. (App 90a-91a) They let their front desk reject our motion and simply said they were unable to locate the lawyer Mr. Messina. Sydney and his Will drafter both live in NYC. They told the Supreme Court of New York State to dismiss my case because the Palmeris are not NYS residents. According to their logic criminals from out of state can commit crimes in New York City and should not be held accountable by our laws. Their strategy worked on all those appellate courts and that is why I was rejected again and again. If Americans allow lawyers to play games by interpreting laws like that there will be no laws and no justice in our country.

How can we recognize their credibly and their affidavits when they ignored the fact like that? Under their intense misleading Judge Mella did not mention a word about Vanguard's flashdrive. Before the hearing ended my counsel mention Vanguard's tape record Mell still ignored it (App 30a-31a)

- **THEY RELY ON AFFIRMATIONS**

They dismissed any documents that they don't like and meanwhile used three lawyers and 7 people to support them by making affirmations or interpreting laws. None of them could tell why Palmeris deserved all Sydney's asset, double of what their aunt, Teresa Field would have got. Curtin is the one who made the most affirmations in this case:

- Sydney embraced the Palmeris like his family members. That is why he gave them all his money (App 88a the last two para)

- Sydney "was the only one to give the instrument to Curtin." Those 10, 15, 20, and 40 means the percentage of his dispositive estate to the Palmeris. (App 87a)
- Curtin switched the 5% from Diana to Victor based on Sydney's indication on the telephone.
- Curtin copied the 2006 provisions to accuse Richard Fields and Kenneth in the 2014 Will and had no reference. He simply attested because Sydney told him to do that (App 88a-89a)
- In the 2006 will, the only Fields family member Lewis Fields had same provision as Victor. In the 2014 will Victor got eventually four million dollars eventually and Lewis got nothing. Curtin had no reference and just accused that Lewis refused to see Sydney. Sydney actually kept pictures Lewis sent to him in 2005.

Curtin admitted that he never read the will out loud and no witnesses were present when he read the will side by side with Sydney. Since he said Sydney could read with a magnifying glass his Will execution was considered dully by judge Mella.

Curtin and his witness attesting that it was an aide who accompanied Sydney to the law office when the will was signed and the beneficiaries were not involved. Curtin's apartment has two bedrooms, one office room, one bed room and the waiting area is his living room. It is impossible that none of them could remember the aide's age, gender, ethnic group, and contact ways. The Judge Mella simply said the aide "appears to have stayed in a separate area". (App 16a line 10-14) She then announced that *"the testimony of the attorney-drafter, which established that the beneficiaries had no direct involvement in the preparation of the execution of the will." (App 14a-15a)*

- Diana told a lie about the first time she met Curtin. Diana said: "I spoke to him at the will signing— sorry I did not say will signing. At the will reading, will reading." She later emphasized it again: "I did not mean to say will-signing, I did not meet him at any will signing." (App 67a) However, Curtin said there was no will reading at all. (App 68a last two para) Diana said she "have no power over any account, he (Sydney) never initiated anything in terms of finances. He told me what to do. She admitted her POA in Vanguard until we mentioned it.

- **THEY ACCUSED ME BUT AVOIDED MENTIONING MY MENTAL STATE**

They knew my mental status but never mentioned it in the court when they attacked me. On March 27, 2017, they requested the court to have an emergency meeting to stop my crazy behavior because I mailed more than 50 letters to them within five days. I lost my mind after a long deposition and told them I would give up. In the letters they gave to the court they mentioned: "During Objectant's initial deposition, Objectant related that he was presently taking psychotropic drugs and that the medication might affect his ability to answer questions and recall events, Objectant testified that he is a diagnosed paranoid schizophrenic." (App166a last para). However when they attacked me for harassing my father they never mentioned my mental state as well as Judge Mella.(App.12a)

In the Will of 2014 Curtin simply type words my father said in 2006. He admit that "I typed it in this affirmation . . . Sydney wanted to be sure that this provision was left in the 2014 will as well as the provision relating to his son, Kenneth." (App 89a)

Blood is thicker than water and time should be able to wash the conflicts between father and sons. I need valid reference but not just affirmation to proof my father still hated his sons 20 years after those harasses and tragedy happened.

- **THEY TOOK ADVANTAGE OF A FAMILY THAT HAD THREE MENTAL PATIENTS**

My father was born one day after my grandfather died on Dec 30, 1918. A flu then killed 26 million people all over the world. A doctor, Groginsky, risked his life to help my family and signed both the death and birth certificates. Born with a sad background my father considered he was the backbone and worked very hard to bring his family up to middle class. Unfortunately his first two wives were psychiatric patients and that made his family fall apart. The first wife Sara lived in a mental hospital since their son, Kenneth was 2 years old. Kenneth left home earlier and his relationship with Sydney was not close.

My mother Gladys was a schoolteacher. She got no alimony from her multimillionaire husband when devoiced. She cried in front of me since I was a helpless three years child. She walked for one hundred blocks in the winter when she put food on a table to feed me like feeding a cat. She constantly cursed and attacked my father and drove me crazy.

She lost her job and became homeless a few times. She received psychiatric treatment at the end of her life. My father's assets mixed with her tears and blood.

1989-1991 before and after Lewis was born, my father met us every week. I ran away 1991 when my father referred me to a mental hospital where they kept me as an inpatient. I believed what my mother said my father should send me to law school instead and I was very upset. My father told me if I walk away I would destroy his hard work for this family in his whole life. Lewis lost his chance to see my father since then. (App 97a-105a)

From 1994 to 1995 I sent pictures to my father and sent threatening notes to my half—brother, Kenneth when I lost my mind. It could be seen from my expressions shown in those pictures (App 195a-197a)

My father did have me arrested during those days. Yet he refused to end the relationship with me and for that reason he lost the court case when he asked for visiting Kenneth's children. He was upset and said this in his biography: Nobody, especially children should be denied any source of healthy love since there is no such thing as too much love. (App 187a). Thing were out of his control and since that Fields family felt apart.

I did not hire a lawyer to sue my father for money. My mother's lawyer ran after my father for money and gave me nothing when he won the case. I never get a chance to explain that to my father. That lawyer stole my money as well as the Palmeris.

I was in and out of mental hospital in the last twenty years and lost my shelter a few times. I never contacted my father again because I did not want to bother him. The Palmeris took advantage of the situation and took all my father's assets. Judge Mella simply accepted their accusations. She described me in this way "He admits that he did not have a relationship with decedent and that he never saw his father for the last 19 years of his life. Moreover, objectant admits that, over the years, he sent his father correspondence and photographs that were harassing or threatening." (App12a)

I am living on SSI now and receiving psychiatric treatment. Acted as Pro Se I have Pia Fields, my son's mother composed this motions. I read, corrected and presented them. Pia pictures my grandmother was watching my grandfather's dead body being moved out and gave my father born birth. She admire the doctor and think of giving this family a hand herself as well. She did not expect that we really need her. She fights and is desponded when the little baby then was robbed in our courtrooms and nobody gave a damn. Things are ugly comparing with what the doctor did one hundred years ago.

CONCLUSIONS

You should review our case and dismiss the 2014 will for the reasons listed below:

- The will execution process was unduly! The Will for a blind man was never read out loud in front of the witnesses. The respondent and her lawyers com- mitted perjury and said Sydney could read. Judge Mella believed it was because a magnifying glass was mentioned by two attesting witnesses.
  - Judge Mella didn't question about the forged initial that resulted in switching the distribution and falsifying the will. She said: "the law doesn't require an initial to make a will valid." (App 6a)
  - Judge Mella simply accepted the will drafter's affirmation and believed a "dispositive terms of the proposed instrument was provided by decedent orally". No video or audiotapes related to the 2014 will were requested. She meanwhile ignored the only audiotapes that recorded the decedent's statement about his vision. She ignored medical report provided by the eye doctor as well.
  - They took advantage of a family that had three mental patients. The appellate courts never reviewed my appeals

even though American law never punish but only help psychiatric patients.

If we win the case we will set up a fund to memorialize doctor Groginsky and my father. We will use the fund to promote ideas about building retirement homes. Pia said compared with the proposal our case is insignificant. For the $100,000 legal fee she paid I allowed her to mention her proposal here. She said if we lose she at least has compensation and ends her worries for this world. Having people like Mella run this country she should not brother. She was the author of a book "Why Life Events are Predestined and How Our Universe Originated" (whydestiny.com). She ties up this case and her proposal together to bet their destiny. She believes what people deserved are fixed in their lives. If they overtake fortunes they have to pay in the other hand, such as having cancer, losing a job, or having sick children who get no chance to enjoy their money. For the nine million dollars assets Sydney had his father and step father die earlier, has two crazy wives, and lost contact with his two sons. For the suffering he had and the donations he tried to make the power that helped him to accumulate those assets allow him to come back as Lewis' son and do things that are more important. We are just chess pieces of the secret power. Below are things that the Fields family might do in the future.

- **Something beyond This Case**

The debt of the US government is over 22 trillion dollars as of today and social security funds will dry up by the year of 2034. America can't, as Donald Trump expects, be great again when the government's debt continues to rise. It is said that over 50% of the government's expenses are related to Social Security, Medicare, Medicaid, and welfare for the low income class.

Proposal about building retirement homes can help us reduce these mandatory expenses. The proposal is outlined below:

Civil society organizations have retired people sign up certain agreements and present their proposal about building living centers. The government will have joint-venture with them to build apartments in the suburb and rent it. The rent will be deducted from tenants' social security checks. A unit that costs $50,000 construction fee can rent for $700 monthly. That means in 30 years an apartment can help the government save $240,000 social security payments. By doing so, the government acts as a landlord instead of merely a social security distributor.

Why would people prefer to move to those centers? In New York City today, people have to pay $800 in maintenance fees monthly for their apartment even when their mortgages are paid off. If they pay that $800 to the center, they at least can have $200,000 in cash from liquidating their apartments plus friends, entertainment, and homecare. Today in New York City, with that kind of living conditions, half of a room cost over $10,000 per month. There a are also centers that provide entertainments during day to low income retirement people. They charge the government $80 for every member per day. Comparing $120-$240 one to one home care expenses every day government considers the $80 is worthy. The retirement centers we mentioned could charge a much lower fee for the reasons listed below:

- The land where these centers are situated cost much less than in the city. Transportation provided by these centers make the suburb as convenient as the city.
- Home care in the center is not provided by aides, but by the tenants. The younger ones keep an eye on the older ones

and build credit for the home care they need in the future. The government no longer creates jobs in home care field and provide the home care service for the same people a few years later. This way, we can eliminate government's expenses relate to home care permanently. A country in north Europe records people's credit for the home care they provide to the other people.
- 3. The government can set up patrol medical teams and monitor people's health in different centers. On that way it can prevent those unnecessary medical cost and save government's Medical and Medicare funds. Centers will recommend internal exercise such as Qigong or Yoga, which aim to prevent illness ahead of time rather than medicating for it after.
- 4. In the centers, middle aged people may need to produce organic food for themselves, work a few hours a day in farms. During other hours, they can sing, dance, cook, play poker, watch TV and attend different classes. People can register with friends or family members who are over 50 years old. They will have their own apartments and can cook their own food as they wish.

Transportation, entertainment and friendships that the center maintain will incentivize people pay the rent they pay in the city even though they live in suburb. That is how profit margins are created. Government get profits from managements that provide by civil society organizations.

We aim not only to set up retirement centers but also promote a new philosophy that happiness is not just related to money. Happiness can be generated from friendships and entertainments. We use new standards to measure success: having good income and earning large amounts of money doesn't always mean success. Successful people are those who spend minimal resources on great joy and spread happiness to people around them. They do not need a highly consumerist society to provide them jobs. They survival on a piece of land there provide food they need. Their happiness arises not from shopping, but from friends and leisure time.

We do not seek profits as our hospitals and pharmaceutical companies do. Today, health insurance costs over 25% of our income and it will eventually bankrupt our government and people. By seeking profit, our country's medical field blackmails scores of people who care about their health. I bring up this topic here because a large portion of government's spending goes toward health care. Obama's reforms just raised funds for health insurance and never challenged the overcharging and unnecessary spending in medical field. Trump at least criticizes the greed of the drug manufacturers even though things he can change is not much. When we, for reducing the government debt, encourage people to substitute their material wants with spiritual needs, we have right to suggest limit the profit of our health system.

Our crisis is so serious that our government must close its doors without rasing debt ceiling once a while and there is 22 trillion dollars debt needs to be paid off. All the Western governments are facing the same problem. Eventually they will be unable to distribute welfare to meet the poor's needs and protests, just like the yellow vest did in French, will break out everywhere.

The capitalist system ignores the gap between the poor and the rich. Over these past decades, conflicts are released by government's welfare system. When debt hit the ceiling capitalism get into a dead road.

Capitalist concepts about market demand, supply, profits and stimulate consumption obviously cannot run this world. Even though it maximizes consuming, jobs that the system can provide are much less than what this world need. The obvious evident is that refugees are running around for jobs and for surviving.

In this proposal, the Government can solve surviving problem by provide 3D shelters, land, entertainment and free time. The basic idea is using spiritual entertainment to substitute people's material demands. Get what we need directly from land. We can use this way to solve the homeless problem in the city. Today, New York City is paying thousands of dollars renting motels for homeless people as well as the federal government who pay rent for section 8 people. We should cut off all those expenses by settling them in the living centers and provide them jobs there. People who have no money to pay rent have to move away from the cities and live in suburb. This arrangement has nothing to do with violating human rights: it's the same as people who have no money to pay for their food should not sit in a restaurant.

We can encourage manufacturers to move back from overseas and set up factories around these centers. By providing shelter, medical services, and entertainment, people would not mind cut off 70% of their salary because 65% of expenses that their salary pay for, shelter and medical insurance, have being solved already.

Again the key point here is encouraging spiritual entertainment (can be either reading the Bible or playing poker) rather than material attainment.

At some point this is socialism because people do the same jobs and get the same pay in the centers. Actually, socialism as an ideology is not that bad, it is just that humans have not implemented it properly in the past century. Things might work this time because we are using totally different ways to fulfill our goal.

- It does not provoke the poor to rob the rich like the communist revolution what happened in the last century. Since there is no fight it has no needs to control people's thinking and violate human rights like a dictatorship governments usually do.
- It is not like what the western government has been doing: collect taxes from the rich or create huge debt to benefit the poor. Our government is no longer a welfare distributor, but a big landlord that cares about profit. It, through joint-venture, invests social security funds on shelters and rents it to people. They either collects rent to cover social security payment or make people work in low salary rate for their shelters.
- It make people work but not just provide welfare. It makes life simple by minimum our desires for material needs. It make life enrich by promoting entertainments and friendship. People are no longer need to fight for market, job, higher salary that the capitalist recommend. They survive in a piece of land with harmony that exist in the bottom of the society.

Besides that, we fulfill our goal not through violent revolution or street riots, but by changing the mindset of our young generations. Tell them that happiness doesn't have to tight up with money, but can be built up on friendship, peace of mind and luxury time. A successful life doesn't mean making high salary and big consumption. Successful means using minimal resources to live a happy life. Bhutan, one of the countries that have the highest happiness index, has a very low GDP. Burma is another country that has a really high happy index and their men retire in their thirties.

How our young people think determines what our world will be. Today's day the unemployment rates for the youths are high in most of the countries. Capitalist system tells people to struggle for good pay job, for beautiful house and cars. However, in reality when our youth cannot even find a job to survive they will become restless and riot in the street. That once happened in Egypt, in Paris, now in Hong Kong, Spain and Chile…Even though they protest for different reasons but in deep of their mind they cannot see the future that the capitalist system promise to them. They feel like losers.

So, it is time to teach them live in a new way. We hope they will understand that live in a piece of land peacefully is better than running in the market finding for job. Hope they will understand that it is not worth to carry enormous debts for a degree from good school and then for a good job. It is stupid that work like a robot and then spend money like an idiot. It is painful for keeping a good job act as "Yes man" all their life. They can live in a simple way because money that capitalist recommend is not the only thing that brings happiness. Nature, friends and luxury times can make life beautiful as well.

With this ideology we can encourage people retire at their fifties and leave 20-30 percent of jobs for the younger generation. This proposal is not solo back up by the government but run by different civil society organizations. People from the same country, college, or religion can sign up for building their own centers. That can avoid conflict between different races or classes. It helps the government to collect rent to offset Social Security payment.

It is said that some colleges in the United State did set up the similar retirement centers for their seniors graduated schoolmate. Members over there live 8 years longer and spent 30% healthy insurance fee lesser than the regular people. There is an organization names CCRC that take care of retirement people. However it obtains financial support from the government but not care about government's pressure.

Hopefully, such centers can get help from businesses such as Amazon, Facebook, Microsoft, and Berkshire Hathaway. In this way we can fulfill the socialist system in a practical and peaceful manner. We do not need to argue for trading deficit, worry for jobs and worry for selling merchandise. We do not need to produce weapons and send troops to fight with socialist countries. Instead, we'll show them how to approach socialist goal through harmonious means, with freedom and democracy.

Respectfully submitted,

RICHARD J. FIELDS

PETITIONER PRO SE
2830 PITKIN AVENUE
BROOKLYN, NY 11208
(718) 235-0900
AUGUST 16, 2019

PETITIONER PRO SE
2830 PITKIN AVENUE
BROOKLYN, NY 11208
(718) 235-0900

AUGUST 16, 2019

The above brief was filed in the U.S Supreme Court and was published as a book, "An Appeal to the U.S Supreme Court and a Proposal to Our President" by Pia Fields.The author could not put all her ideas into the brief because of its 9,000 word limitation. The following additional explanation is for the President.

In 2020 the U.S government's debt reached 27 trillion dollars. The government debt, the trade deficit, health insurance and welfare costs are jobs that all U.S presidents have to face.

It has been reported that the winning Democrat administration has promised to provide free housing for the poor in the suburbs; to provide free education and free health insurance to all Americans. They cannot tell us where to get the funds to support their dreams but it seems certain that they will increase business taxes. Such policy will stop manufactures moving back from overseas and keep the trade deficit high. The Democratic Party did care about distributing welfare, collecting tax money from the left hand and spending it with the right hand.

Republican, Donald Trump did not do better than the Democrats. He said he will make America great and the debt he created for us is more than any president. He decreased business taxes. Tax revenue lost is more than the benefit that our society obtained from increased employment. Trump increased import taxes but this expense was transferred to U.S consumers or in some cases US business in China. Many American manufactures refused to move back to the United State because of the high salary rate they have to pay.

Trump made America hate China and simply claimed that the China stole 300 to 400 billion dollars through the trade surplus. This surplus is merchandise market prices that include material costs and manufacturing profit. United States has 30,000 manufacturers making things in China for sale in the United States. Records shows that the Chinese actually only gain $25 on an Apple iPhone that has value of $1,000. Even though the 300 to 400 billion dollars are all Chinese products their net profit is less than 10 billion dollars, 1-2%. Besides that, most of U.S businesses sell their products in China directly and never report that to the U.S customs.In addition, the U.S customs data did not include money that the Chinese students and tours spent in the United States. For that reason, the Chinese would never spend 300-400 billion dollars to purchase U.S products but rather end the trading with U.S. They will exchange their products for raw materials in the market directly instead of saving U.S. dollars.

The Chinese did not only ignore Trump's blackmail in the trading issue they did not believe U.S slogans about democracy as well.Wars in Iraq and Libya overthrew leaders who planned to stop using dollars for oil trading. People of these countries did not have better lives after wars for democracy and freedom. I discuss the relationship between China and U.S for reminding the U.S. president that attacking China could not lead Americans to go anywhere. We need practical ways to reduce our debt, reduce our salary but not coerce China by threatening.

Actually, it is not China or the U.S manufactures that put America into debt. It is the capitalist consumption ideology that misled us. People need high salaries to maintain their big spending. People who cannot make enough money would rely on the government. It is the high healthcare cost, public welfare, social security and military expense that causes the government's high debt. Our Government should arrange jobs and shelters for them but not provide a free lunch. We should keep capitalist concepts about investment and profit return. We should make the economy grow but not simply collect taxes with the left hand and then distribute it with the right hand.

Things we can do are as below:

1) For investing in social security we can provide living centers in suburban areas for retired people. The Center's will provide different kinds of entertainment such as parties, sports, games and social activities. The Center's transportation service will make people feel that they are living in the city. The Center's will let the younger inhabitants keep an eye on the older ones in exchange for the same

services when they get old. Inhabitants taking care of each other can eliminate home care budgets from our government. Government's patrol medical team will give inhabitants regular check-ups to prevent being over charged by private doctors. This kind of facility in New York City currently costs $5000 for a shared room. The new Center's will only charge $700 for an apartment and rent will be deducted from inhabitants' social security checks. To support retired people, the government can spend thirty thousand dollars on low cost housing units. The government can then make two hundred thousand dollars in rental income over thirty years. By investing in realistic fields our government can become a big landlord and prevent social security systems collapse.

2) We can reduce public assistance expenditure and salary expense by setting up the above living centers. It needs to connect the living centers with manufacturers or farms.People on public welfare will work for their housing and living expenses. The centers owned by both the government and the private sector, will provide free health care, day care, transportation and entertainment. Since these benefits will equal 80% of income, manufacturers will pay 20% of salary. This Government welfare fund is use to build up housing and help lower salary expense. Private sector employment can also reduce the government welfare expense.

This Center can also connect with farms for help settling illegal immigrants. Farms can offer employment to immigrants. If governments worldwide help their immigrants to survive in this way refugees will work and be respected. Again people's consumption is low but they have enough time and ways to entertain themselves. People in Burma and Nepal in Asia are all living this way and their "Happy index" is higher than in many countries.

Having a low income does not mean having a sad life.I grew up in China. From 1955- 1962 my father was a doctor working for a ship builder. His salary was 120¥ ($20) monthly, about four times people's average income at that time. Rent was 8¥ ($1.30) monthly and our tuition was 3¥ ($0.50) for a semester. Commute time was short. People played poker or basketball after finishing work. Life was happy if there were no political movements or thought reforming campaigns.

In China today, many manufacturers provide dorms to their workers and pay relative low salary. It is said that Israel has similar farms to settle people who need help. There are a few U.S universities that have set up retirement homes for their alumnus. Inhabitants' lives are 8 years longer and medical spending is 30% less.

Management is crucial in these kind of centers. Government can let colleges be involved. Encouraging students to contact potential tenants, building contractors and looking for charity funds. Setting up a center like that is a big challenge. Students who major in business management, art, computer, agriculture, social studies and medicine will have chances to practice what they learn. Learning how to manage society and how to deal with people, not only dealing with their text books. This is Mao's idea in China many years ago. He hoped students can learn and do different things in a special school. It failed because it had no funds and no need. If this idea can help U.S government cut down big deficit on public welfare and make factories move back why not try? Government can make youths do something for society before releasing education funds or scholarships to them. One fund approaching two goals is good for both parties.

Government can also use medical funds to build up its own medical teams. Giving potential students scholarships and letting them work for society afterward and give them a fair salary rate.

Another socialist principle our government should adopt is to limit the profits of drug and oil companies. Suspending their license if they do not follow the rules.

Insurance company functions should be reevaluated. The demand for the whole society to compensate victims is not fair. This is a big burden for our economy. For preventing accidents we can suspend licenses instead of giving out unreasonable high compensation. The Centers I mentioned above will not have an insurance budget. Inhabitants have to give up law suits before being registered.

The last thing I want to mention is the U.S military budget which is equal the total of the first nine countries' spending in the world. Weapons we make were never used and they will bring nothing good for our world when they are used. Huge military budgets did not make American's lives better than countries that have no military spending.

We will not have enemies if we used socialist way to settle people's lives. We will not have enemies in this world and we will not need a military budget.

In general, the difference between my proposal and traditional socialism is:

We do not need violence or revolution; we do not rob the rich to benefit the poor; we do not force people to reform their thoughts. We do not give government officers privilege to corrupt.Inhabitants have freedom to move in and move out with their family members or friends.

The difference between my proposal and the capitalism is: we do not encourage unnecessary consumption but recommend simple life. We do not consider making good money is success. We believe success means spending the least resource for the most pleasure and being able to make people around you happy. We will no longer work like a robot and spend money like a fool. Japan's youth has trend of reducing their desires. When our new generation changes their life goals and changes their demands the whole world will be changed. That is the way we fulfill our goal. We meanwhile expect our government to do what capitalists do, accumulate capital through investments for the benefit of society.

I forward my proposals to reduce government spending on social security, healthcare, home care, public assistance and the military, up to 30% of the United States total annual budget. The whole world, particularly China, see potential US economic crisis, and devaluation of the US currency if the US Government do not address these problems.

APPENDIX TABLE OF CONTENTS

APPENDIX A.
OPINIONS, ORDERS, COURT HEARINGS AND OBJECTIONS

Order of the Court of Appeals for the State of
New York (April 2, 2019) 1a

Order of the Supreme Court for the County of
New York Granting Motion to Dismiss
Complaint (January 31, 2019) 3a

Order of the Appellate Division of the Supreme
Court Dismissing the Motion to Restore the
Appeal (December 27, 2018) 4a

Order of the Appellate Division of the Supreme
Court Dismissing the Appeal
(September 25, 2018) 6a

Decree of Probate
(July 20, 2018) 8a

Decision and Order of the Surrogate's Court of
New York (March 26, 2018) 12a

Order of Court of Appeals for the State of
New York Denying Motion for Reargument
(June 27, 2019) 20a

Objections to Probate
(June 3, 2016) 21a

Transcript about the Hearing in Surrogate's
Court—Relevant Excerpts (March 20, 2018) .. 25a

APPENDIX B.

DOCTOR'S NOTE & TRANSCRIPTS OF TELEPHONE RECORDINGS FROM VANGUARD

Subpoena Duces Tecum to Dr. Janet Searle
(June 5 and June 20, 2017) 34a

Objectant's Subpoena to Vanguard
(February 21, 2017) 46a

Vanguard Response to Subpoena
(March 17, 2017) 49a

Objectant Forwarding Vanguard's USB to
Petitioner (March 24, 2016) 53a

Decedent's Agent Authority to Teresa's Vanguard
Account (March 25, 2014) 54a

Vanguard Telephone Transcript
(October 1, 2014) 55a

Vanguard Telephone Transcripts
—Relevant Excerpts... 59a

Letter from Authorization Sydney Fields to
Jeffrey Kern 64a

APPENDIX C.

PERJURY ABOUT SYDNEY'S VISION

Testimony of Diana Palmieri 66a

Testimony of Suzanne Marie Lehman 73a

Testimony of Jill Curtin 76a

Testimony of E. Curtin 78a

Return of Documents to Richard Chen
(August 24, 2018) 90a

APPENDIX D.
DEPOSITION FOR PIA FIELDS & DATA SHE PROVIDED

Deposition for Pia Fields and Her Data 93a

Pia Fields Provides in Deposition
(Exhibit Three) 97a

APPENDIX E.
DOCUMENTS WITH FORGERY AND MISTAKES

Curt Bagget Handwriting Analysis
(October 13, 2017) 107a

Last Will and Testament of Sydney H. Fields 111a

Check Images 114a

Curt Bagget Curriculum Vitae 117a

Check Images 120a

Testator's Handwritten Note for the Probate Bill
(October 8, 2013) 121a

Curtin's Scratch Paper for Probated Will 124a

APPENDIX F.
SYDNEY'S THREE WILLS

May 2, 1997 Will 130a

July 27, 2006 Will 137a

Backup Document for the Will 2006
    (Handwritten) 144a

Last Will and Testament of Sydney H. Fields
    (October 6, 2014) 147a

APPENDIX G.

CREDIBILITY OF RESPONDENT AND HER LAWYERS

Affirmation in Support of Motion for
    Summary Judgment (April 19, 2016) 158a

Letter from Martin to Laubscher
    (March 27, 2017) 164a

Letter from Dr. Mihailescu and Dr. Giove
    (April 16, 2019) 168a

APPENDIX H.

THE FAMILY HISTORY OF SYDNEY FIELDS

Letter from Attorney Messina to Attorney Chen
    (April 16, 2019) 171a

Opinion of the Superior Court of New Jersey,
    Chancery Division (May 14, 1998) 172a

Typewritten Note 186a

Sydney Fields Brief Autobiography
    (Translation of handwritten document) 187a

Photos 189a

TPO Order
  (March 18, 1996) 192a
TPO Order
  (April 16, 1996) 194a
Family Photo 196a

APPENDIX A
Opinions, Orders, Court Hearings and Objections

App.1a

ORDER OF THE COURT OF APPEALS FOR THE STATE OF NEW YORK (APRIL 2, 2019)

STATE OF NEW YORK
COURT OF APPEALS

In the Matter of
Will of SYDNEY H. FIELDS,

Deceased,

RICHARD FIELDS,

Appellant,

v.

DIANA PALMERI,

Respondent.

Mo. No. 2019-125

Before: Hon. Janet DiFIORE, Chief Judge, presiding.

Appellant having appealed and moved for leave to appeal to the Court of Appeals in the above cause;

Upon the papers filed and due deliberation, it is

ORDERED, on the Court's own motion, that the appeal, insofar as taken from the September 2018

App.2a

Appellate Division order, is dismissed, without costs, as untimely (*see* CPLR 5513[a]); and it is further

ORDERED, that the appeal, insofar as taken from the December 2018 Appellate Division order, is dismissed, without costs, upon the ground that such order does not finally determine the proceeding within the meaning of the Constitution; and it is further

ORDERED, that the motion, insofar as it seeks leave to appeal from the September 2018 Appellate Division order, is dismissed as untimely (*see* CPLR 5513 [b]); and it is further

ORDERED, that the motion, insofar as it seeks leave to appeal from the December 2018 Appellate Division order, is dismissed upon the ground that such order does not finally determine the proceeding within the meaning of the Constitution.

/s/ John P. Asiello
Clerk of the Court

App.3a

ORDER OF THE SUPREME COURT FOR THE COUNTY OF NEW YORK GRANTING MOTION TO DISMISS COMPLAINT (JANUARY 31, 2019)

SUPREME COURT OF THE STATE OF NEW YORK
NEW YORK COUNTY

FIELDS, RICHARD,

vs

PALMERI, DIANA,

Index Number: 101305/2018
Sequence Number: 002

Before: Barbara JAFFE, J.S.C.

Upon the foregoing papers, it is ordered

Defendants' motion to dismiss the complaint is granted, as this court has no appellate authority over surrogate's court. Plaintiff's remedy is an appeal to the Appellate Division.

/s/ Barbara Jaffe
J.S.C.

Dated: 1/30/19

1. Check One: Case Disposed
2. Check as Appropriate: Motion is Granted

App.4a

ORDER OF THE APPELLATE DIVISION OF THE SUPREME COURT DISMISSING THE MOTION TO RESTORE THE APPEAL (DECEMBER 27, 2018)

SUPREME COURT OF THE STATE OF NEW YORK
FIRST JUDICIAL DEPARTMENT,
COUNTY OF NEW YORK

Probate Proceeding,
Will of SYDNEY H. FIELDS,

Deceased.

RICHARD FIELDS,

Objectant-Appellant,

-against-

DIANA PALMERI,

Respondent-Respondent.

Surrogate's Court M-5489
File No. 2016-111

Before: Hon. David FRIEDMAN, Justice Presiding,
Barbara R. KAPNICK, Marcy L. KAHN,
Ellen GESMER, Cynthia S. KERN, Justices.

An appeal having been taken by objectant-appellant Richard J. Fields from an order of the Surrogates

App.5a

Court, New York County, entered on or about March 26, 2018,

And an order of this Court having been entered on September 25, 2018 (M-3860/M-4076), granting petitioner's cross motion to dismiss the appeal (M-3860) and denying objectant-appellant's motion to reverse the decree and to stay the petitioner from liquidating the estate assets (M-4076),

And objectant-appellant having moved to restore the appeal,

Now, upon reading and filing the papers with respect to the motion, and due deliberation having been had thereon,

It is ordered that the motion is denied.

ENTERED:

/s/ {Illegible}
Clerk

App.6a

ORDER OF THE APPELLATE DIVISION OF THE SUPREME COURT DISMISSING THE APPEAL (SEPTEMBER 25, 2018)

SUPREME COURT OF THE STATE OF NEW YORK
FIRST JUDICIAL DEPARTMENT,
COUNTY OF NEW YORK

Probate Proceeding,
Will of SYDNEY H. FIELDS,

Deceased.

Surrogate's Court M-3860, M-4076
File No. 2016-111

Before: Hon. David FRIEDMAN, Justice Presiding,
Barbara R. KAPNICK, Marcy L. KAHN,
Ellen GESMER, Cynthia S. KERN, Justices.

An appeal having been taken by objectant-appellant Richard J. Fields from an order of the Surrogates Court, New York County, entered on or about March 26, 2018, and said appeal having been perfected,

And appellant Richard J. Fields having moved to reverse the probate decree, and to stay petitioner from liquidating the estate assets (M-4076),

And petitioner-respondent having cross-moved to dismiss the aforesaid appeal or, in the alternative, to strike certain portions of the appellants appendix and brief, to adjourn the appeal to the November 2018 Term, and for other relief (M-3860),

App. 7a

Now, upon reading and filing the papers with respect to the motion and cross motion, and due deliberation having been had thereon,

It is ordered that the cross motion by petitioner is granted and the appeal is dismissed (M-3860). The motion by appellant to reverse the probate decree and stay petitioner from liquidating the estate assets is denied (M-4076).

ENTERED: September 25, 2018

/s/ {Illegible}
Clerk

App.8a

DECREE OF PROBATE
(JULY 20, 2018)

NEW YORK COUNTY SURROGATE'S COURT

Probate Proceeding,
Will of SYDNEY H. FIELDS,

Deceased.

File No.: 2016-111

Before: Rita MELLA, Judge of the Surrogate's Court

A Petition for Probate having been filed by Diana Palmeri ("Petitioner") dated December 17, 2015 seeking a Decree admitting the Last Will and Testament of Sydney H. Fields dated October 6, 2014 to probate and the issuance of letters testamentary to Petitioner; and

a Citation having been issued in connection with such Petition, and jurisdiction having been obtained over the necessary parties to said proceeding; and

an application having been filed by Diana Palmeri dated June 6, 2016 seeking the issuance of preliminary letters testamentary to Petitioner; and

Preliminary letters testamentary having been issued to Diana Palmeri on July 19, 2016; and

Petitioner having appeared by her attorneys, Edward R. Curtin. Esq., co-counsel Jules Martin Haas,

App.9a

Esq., and trial counsel Albert V. Messina Jr. Esq., of Novick & Associates, P.C., and

Richard Fields, having initially appeared by his counsel Dehai Zhang, Esq., and later by Richard Alan Chen, Esq., and

Objections to Probate with Jury Demand dated February 24, 2016 having been filed by Richard Fields, alleging that the October 6, 2014 Will was not duly executed, that Sydney H. Fields did not possess the requisite testamentary capacity to execute the Will, that Sydney H. Fields did not know or understand the contents of the Will and that the Will was the product of fraud, duress and undue influence, and

the parties by their respective counsel having engaged in SCPA § 1404 examinations and CPLR Article 31 discovery; and

Petitioner having filed a motion for summary judgment pursuant to CPLR § 3212 dated November 28, 2017 seeking dismissal of the Objections to Probate filed by Richard Fields; and

Petitioner having filed an affirmation in support of motion for summary judgment of Jules Martin Haas, Esq. dated November 28, 2017, including deposition transcripts and other documents annexed thereto as exhibits, the affirmation of Edward R. Curtin, Esq., dated November 27, 2017, the affidavit of Diana Palmeri, sworn to on November 28, 2017, the affidavit of Adrienne Lawler sworn to on September 14, 2016, that affidavit of Arthur Fishelman sworn to on June 12, 2017, the affidavit of Stuart Michael sworn to on September 14, 2016, the affidavit of Irving Rothbart sworn to on September 14, 2016, the affidavit of William McAllister sworn to on September 30, 2016,

App.10a

the affidavit of Gloria Madero sworn to on July 12, 2017 and a memorandum of law in support of motion of Albert V. Messina Jr. dated November 28, 2017; and

Objectant Richard Fields having submitted an affirmation with legal citations in opposition to motion for summary judgment of Richard Alan Chen, Esq., dated January 22, 2018, with exhibits annexed thereto, and an affidavit from Richard Fields sworn to on January 22, 2018; and

Petitioner having submitted a reply affirmation of Jules Martin Haas, Esq., dated February 23, 2018, with exhibits annexed thereto; and

the allegations of the parties having been heard, and oral argument of the motion for summary judgment having been heard before the Court on March 20, 2018, and upon all the pleadings and proceedings heretofore filed and had herein, and after due deliberation the Court having granted granting Petitioner's motion for summary judgment and dismissing the objections to probate on March 20, 2018, and the Court having rendered its written decision dated March 26, 2018;

NOW, upon motion of Novick & Associates, P.C., as attorneys for Petitioner, it is hereby

ORDERED, ADJUDGED and DECREED, that the written instrument dated October 6, 2014 offered for probate as the Last Will and Testament of Sydney H. Fields herein be and the same is hereby admitted to probate; and it is further

ORDERED, ADJUDGED and DECREED that letters testamentary shall issue to Diana Palmeri

App.11a

upon qualification and without the posting of a bond; and it is further

ORDERED, ADJUDGED and DECREED that preliminary letters testamentary dated July 19, 2016 are hereby revoked, and it is further

ORDERED, ADJUDGED and DECREED that a judgment in favor of Petitioner for costs and disbursements has been DENIED in the Courts exercise of discretion.

<u>Jury</u>
Surrogate Court

App.12a

DECISION AND ORDER OF THE SURROGATE'S COURT OF NEW YORK (MARCH 26, 2018)

SURROGATE'S COURT OF THE STATE OF NEW YORK, COUNTY OF NEW YORK

In the Matter of the Probate Proceeding, Will of SYDNEY H. FIELDS,

Deceased.

File No.: 2016-111

Before: Rita MELLA, Judge of the Surrogate's Court

MELLA, S.:

At the call of the calendar on March 20, 2018, the court granted proponent's motion for summary determination, dismissed the objections, and directed probate of the October 6, 2014 instrument offered as the will of decedent Sydney Fields. Objectant is the child of decedent, and he admits that he did not have a relationship with decedent and that he never saw his father for the last 19 years of his life. Moreover, objectant admits that, over the years, he sent his father correspondence and photographs that were harassing or threatening.[1]

---

[1] Objectant stated in opposition to this motion: "I wrote and sent harassing letters and photos to my father, and also to my half-brother . . . [who did not appear in this proceeding], and Orders of Protection were issued against me and criminal

App.13a

Decedent explicitly disinherited objectant in the instrument offered for probate,[2] which, instead, benefits members of the family of decedent's spouse, who was not objectant's mother. Decedent's spouse died before him in September of 2014, which lead decedent to seek to revise his penultimate will—from 2006—that had benefited her, but which also had disinherited objectant in terms identical to those used in the 2014 instrument. The attorney-drafter of decedent's two prior wills was also the drafter of the 2014 instrument here offered for probate, and he confirms that, despite decedent having been in his 90s, his mental faculties were intact and that it was decedent alone in a meeting who informed the attorney-drafter of who he wanted to benefit with his estate and in what percentages.

On the merits, the attestation clause in the instrument, the contemporaneous affidavit of the attesting witnesses, as well as the sworn testimony of these witnesses and the attorney-drafter, established a prima facie case for probate (*Matter of Schlaeger*, 74 AD3d. 405 [1st Dept. 2010]). In response, objectant failed to demonstrate, through admissible evidence, the existence of a material question of fact requiring a trial on any of the objections on which he claims

---

charges were filed against me. I am not proud I did that" (Objectant's Affidavit in Opposition, dated January 22, 2018, ¶ 11).

[2] Article FIFTH(b) of the instrument states: "Because my son [objectant] hired a lawyer to sue me for money and because I had to have him arrested and brought to court for harassment of me and my wife, Teresa[,] I deliberately make no provision for him in this Will and it is my intention that he receive no part of my estate."

App.14a

probate should be denied (*Zuckerman v. City of New York*, 49 NY2d. 557 [1980]). He objected that decedent lacked testamentary capacity, that the will was the product of undue influence, duress, mistake or fraud, and that it was not duly executed.

As to mental capacity, all the medical records, the affidavit of the attesting witnesses and their testimony from the SCPA 1404 examinations, as well as the affidavits of several neighbors and friends confirm the lucidity and mental acuity of decedent both before and after the will execution, despite his advanced age and his having some visual impairment. No evidence submitted by objectant raises a question of whether decedent could hold in his mind the nature and extent of his assets, the identity of the natural objects of his bounty, and the consequences of executing the will, which is the traditional test for determining testamentary capacity (*Matter of Kumstar*, 66 NY2d. 691 [1985]; *Matter of Khazaneh*, 15 Misc 3d. 515 [Sur Ct, NY County 2006]).

Regarding undue influence, proponent's proof established that this was a natural will, benefiting members of the family of decedent's spouse, with whom decedent was close and whom he considered his family. In opposition, objectant had to show, through evidence in admissible form, that the persons alleged to have unduly influenced decedent to make this will had the motive and opportunity to do so, together with some evidence, circumstantial or otherwise, indicating that undue influence was actually exercised on decedent (*Matter of Greenwald*, 47 AD3d 1036 [3d Dept 2008]). Objectant, however, provided no evidence that the will's beneficiaries had the opportunity to exercise undue influence or that they

App.15a

did so in light of the testimony of the attorney-drafter, which established that the beneficiaries had no direct involvement in the preparation or execution of the will (*see Matter of Camac*, 300 AD2d 11 [1st Dept 2002]).

Objectant offered no evidence of duress—a wrongful threat precluding the exercise of free will—allegedly inflicted on decedent (*Matter of Guttenplan*, 222 AD2d 255 [1st Dept 1995]), nor any evidence of mistake (*Matter of Seelig*, 302 AD2d 721 [3d Dept 2003]). Objectant also failed to provide evidence of a misrepresentation made to decedent for the purposes of inducing him to make a will that he would not otherwise have made, as would be necessary to create a question of fact as to a fraud claim (*Matter of Schwartz*, 154 AD3d 540 [1st Dept 2017]; *Matter of Capuano*, 93 AD3d 666 [2d Dept 2012]).[3] These objections were thus dismissed.

Finally, as to the will's execution, the claimed failure of the attesting witnesses to remember all its details are insufficient to rebut the presumption of regularity in the execution of a will (*Matter of Collins*, 60 NY2d 466 [1983]). When read in its entirety, the deposition testimony of the two attesting witnesses supports the conclusion that the signature on the instrument is decedent's and that decedent executed the instrument with full awareness of what he was doing and in compliance with all statutory require-

---

[3] Objectant's opposition papers state that he has not had an opportunity to depose the concierge at decedent's building, who provided an affidavit in support of the motion. However, after submitting his opposition to the motion, objectant filed a note of issue and certificate of readiness with the court stating that all discovery has concluded.

ments (EPTL 3-2.1). Additionally, when the execution was supervised by an attorney and when there is a contemporaneous affidavit of the attesting witnesses reciting the facts of due execution, as is the case here, a presumption of proper execution arises (*Matter of Natale*, 158 AD3d. 579 [1st Dept 2018]).[4] Here, the facts that the attesting witnesses could not confirm whether decedent had his magnifying glass that day (the attorney-drafter and one of the witnesses testified that he did) and could not provide a description of the **aide who accompanied decedent to the will execution, but who appears to have stayed in a separate waiting area, were insufficient to rebut the presumption under the circumstances presented (*see id.*).**

The fact that decedent had some visual impairment, even to the point of "legal" blindness as objectant argues, does not change this conclusion because blind persons may make wills (*Matter of McCabe*, 75 Misc 35, 36 [Sur Ct, NY County 1911])). **Here, the attorney-drafter testified that the dispositive terms of the proposed instrument were provided to him by decedent himself and that he confirmed those dispositive provisions of the will orally to decedent shortly before execution.** Moreover, the fact that the attorney-drafter had to mark the signature line at the end of the instrument with "X's," as requested by decedent, but the attorney-drafter did not mark "X's" where decedent's

---

[4] The fact that the attorney supervising the will execution corrected the date by hand in the text of this affidavit does not alter this analysis. Even if, for the sake of argument, it did, due execution of the will was confirmed by the testimony of the attesting witnesses and the attorney-drafter at their SCP A 1404 examinations, transcripts of which were provided in support of the motion.

App.17a

initials on the preceding pages of the will should be, is not suspicious (*see id.*). The last page of the will has both the signature line for the testator and signature lines for the attesting witnesses. Accordingly, the only inference that can reasonably be drawn from the fact that the attorney-drafter marked the testator's signature line with "X's" is that the testator wanted to be sure to execute the document correctly in spite of his visual impairment.

The remaining evidence on which objectant relies to support his claim that the will was not duly executed is the sworn-to "Letter of Opinion" of a claimed handwriting expert,[5] which merely concludes that "a different person authored the initials of SHF" on the first page of the will[6] offered for probate from the person who signed the will. **This letter does not conclude that decedent's signature at the end of the will is a forgery, or even that it might be (*see Matter of Dane*, 32 AD3d 1233 [4th Dept 2006]).**

---

[5] Movant contests the expertise of the person making the report, pointing to the fact that Federal courts have rejected him as an expert in handwriting. Movant cites the following cases in this regard: *Balimunkwe v. Bank of Am., NA.*, 2017 US App. Lexis 19875 (6th Cir., Jan. 17, 2017); *U.S. v. Revels*, 2012 US Dist. Lexis 65069, at *22 (ED Tenn., May 9, 2012); and *Dracz v. Am. Gen. Life Ins. Co.*, 426 F.Supp.2d 1373, 1378-379 (MD Ga 2006).

[6] The will is three pages long, and only a copy of the first page of the proffered will is attached to the opinion letter reporting that the initials on it are not from the person who signed the instrument at the end. No opinion is offered as to initials on its second page, and the court considers this opinion letter as addressing only the initials on the first page of the proffered will.

App.18a

Even if the court were to consider this letter an affidavit of an expert, there is no requirement that a testator initial the pages of a will for it to be valid (*see* EPTL 3-2.1[a][1]). Instead, all that is required in this regard is that it have been signed "at the end thereof" (*id.*). The opinion letter is not addressed to the real issue—whether it is decedent's signature at the end of the will—a fact that objectant does not contest with competent evidence (*Matter of Herman*, 289 AD2d 239, 239-240 [2d Dept 2001] [objectant's burden is to provide particulars in order to create issue of fact on a claim of forgery]; *Matter of Taylor*, 32 Misc 3d 1277(A), 2011 NY Slip Op 51440(U), at *4 [Sur Ct, Bronx County 2011], *citing Matter of Di Scala*, 131 Misc 2d 532, 534 [Sur Ct, Westchester County 1986]; *see also Celaj v. Cornell*, 144 AD3d 590 [1st Dept 2016] [expert report on collateral issue does not require denial of summary judgment]). Thus, this letter is insufficient in this instance to resist summary dismissal of the objection that the will was not duly executed (*see Matter of James*, 17 AD3d 366 [2d Dept 2005]; *see also Kopeloff v. Arctic Cat. Inc.*, 84 AD3d 890, 891 [2d Dept 2011]; *Murphy v. Conner*, 84 NY2d 969, 972 [1994]). Finally, objectant's surmise that, "it is possible the first two pages of the Will were exchanged for other unknown pages" after the will was executed is mere speculation, insufficient to create an issue of fact requiring a trial (*see Matter of Weltz*, 16 AD3d 428 [2d Dept 2005]).

In examining all the evidence, the court determined that the October 6, 2014 instrument is valid and genuine and should be admitted to probate (*Collins*, 60 NY2d at 473; *see* SCPA 1408).

App.19a

Accordingly, the court granted proponent's motion for summary judgment, and the objections to probate were dismissed.

This decision, together with the transcript of the March 20, 2018 proceedings, constitutes the order of the court.

Settle probate decree.

/s/ Rita Mella
Judge of the Surrogate's Court

Dated: March 26, 2018

App.20a

ORDER OF COURT OF APPEALS FOR THE STATE OF NEW YORK DENYING MOTION FOR REARGUMENT (JUNE 27, 2019)

STATE OF NEW YORK
COURT OF APPEALS

In the Matter of
Will of SYDNEY H. FIELDS,

Deceased,

RICHARD FIELDS,

Appellant,

v.

DIANA PALMERI,

Respondent.

Mo. No. 2019-435

Before: Hon. Janet DiFIORE, Chief Judge, presiding.

Appellant having moved for reargument in the above cause;

Upon the papers filed and due deliberation, it is ORDERED, that the motion is denied.

/s/ John P. Asiello
Clerk of the Court

App.21a

OBJECTIONS TO PROBATE
(JUNE 3, 2016)

SURROGATE'S COURT OF THE STATE OF
NEW YORK, COUNTY OF NEW YORK

Probate Proceeding,
Will of SYDNEY H. FIELDS,

Deceased.

File No.: 2016-111

The Attorney General of the State of New York, appearing on behalf of the ultimate beneficiaries of gifts for charitable purposes pursuant to Article 8 of the Estates, Powers and Trusts Law, contests and objects to the probate of the paper writing dated October 6, 2014, offered for probate as the Last Will and Testament of Sydney H. Fields, the above-named decedent, and alleges, upon information and belief, the following:

1. The paper writing offered for probate is not the Last Will and Testament of Sydney H. Fields in that the decedent was not competent to make a Will and on October 6, 2014, the decedent was not of sound mind or memory.

2. The paper writing alleged to be the Last Will and Testament of Sydney H. Fields was not freely or voluntarily made or executed by Sydney H. Fields as his Last Will and Testament, but that paper writing

App.22a

purporting to be his Will was obtained, and the subscription and publication of that paper writing, if in fact it was subscribed and published by him, was procured by duress and undue influence practiced upon the decedent by Diana Palmeri, Olga Palmeri, Victor Palmeri, Jr., Cynthia Palmeri, or by some other person or persons acting independently or in concert or privity with Diana Palmeri, Olga Palmeri, Victor Palmeri, Jr., Cynthia Palmeri, or others whose names are presently unknown to the objectant.

3. The paper writing alleged to be the Last Will and Testament of Sydney H. Fields was not freely and voluntarily made or executed by decedent, and the writing was obtained, and its subscription and publication, if it was in fact subscribed and published by decedent, was caused or procured by actual or constructive fraud practiced upon decedent by Diana Palmeri, Olga Palmeri, Victor Palmeri, Jr., Cynthia Palmeri, or by some other person or persons acting independently or in concert or privity Diana Palmeri, Olga Palmeri, Victor Palmeri, Jr., Cynthia Palmeri, or others whose names are presently unknown to the objectant.

4. The paper writing alleged to be the Last Will and Testament of Sydney H. fields was not duly executed by Theodore Matthew Pechacek as required by law.

5. The signature purporting to have been subscribed by Sydney H. Fields at the end of the paper writing alleged to be the Last Will and Testament Sydney H. Fields was forged and written by Diana Palmeri, Olga Palmeri, Victor Palmeri, Jr., Cynthia Palmeri, or by some other person or persons acting independently or in concert or privity with Diana

App.23a

Palmeri, Olga Palmeri, Victor Palmeri, Jr., Cynthia Palmeri, or others whose names are presently unknown to the objectant.

6. A trial by jury of the issues raised by these Objections is hereby demanded.

WHEREFORE, the objectant requests that this proceeding be dismissed, with prejudice, and costs, and that the probate of the paper so propounded be denied and that the objectant be granted such other and further relief as this Court deems just and proper.

      Eric T. Schneiderman
      Attorney General of the
      State of New York

     By: /s/ Lisa Barbieri
       Assistant Attorney General
       120 Broadway
       New York, NY 10271
       Telephone: 212-416-8396

Dated: New York, New York
    June 3, 2016

To:

  Edward R. Curtin, Esq.
  Law Offices of Edward R. Curtin. Esq.
  220 West 71st Street, Suite 31
  New York, NY 10023-3720

App.24a

Richard Alan Chen, Esq.
Law Offices of Richard Allan Chen, Esq.
41-60 Main Street, Suite 208
Flushing, New York 11355

App.25a

TRANSCRIPT ABOUT THE HEARING IN SURROGATE'S COURT—RELEVANT EXCERPTS (MARCH 20, 2018)

SURROGATE'S COURT OF THE STATE OF NEW YORK, COUNTY OF NEW YORK

In the Matter of the estate of
SIDNEY H . FIELDS

Deceased.

File No . 2016-111

Before: The Honorable Rita MELLA, Surrogate Court Judge

[March 20, 2018 Transcript, p. 21]

. . . objectant that the prior will had and all of the witnesses' testimony as far as execution was full and consistent with due execution and testamentary capacity. So, I don't think that there's an issue there whatsoever, Judge.

Now, as far as the issue that counsel, for a time I'm just going to talk about some of the issues that objectant's counsel raised. The X's on the will, all right, there are X's next to the decedent's signature that the decedent, from the testimony, asked the attorney draftsperson to put on the signature line. Those X's don't appear on the pages where the decedent initialed the will. Well,

App.26a

first of all, there's no requirement in the law that a will be initialed and the fact that there are no X's to initial the will on the will pages, there's no particular line where you have to sign.

And, in fact, the fact that the decedent wanted to sign on the right line, all right, to make sure that his signature was in the right place, I think **is an important factor. And the fact that the decedent had a limited—this limited eyesight, again, Judge, is a non-issue. All right? There's nothing to prevent a person who has limited eyesight from signing a will. All of the testimony shows that the will was gone over completely with the attorney draftsperson, that he completely understood that the decedent is the one who basically guided what to put in his will and he signed his will under perfect circumstances. There's no question as to how any of that occurred.** So, I think all of this, again, Judge, is a non-issue. It's just a distraction, all right, because there is no question as question as counsel admitted about testamentary capacity. There is no issue about the way this will was executed. In fact, there is no issue of undue influence. In fact, counsel didn't even refer to undue influence. There are no issues about how any of these matters came to pass.

What we have is a son who had no contact with his father, who threatened his father, and who the—whose father left him out of the will for a very specific purpose that's—that's designated in the will.

As far as, you know, again, these are very side matters, Judge. Counsel mentioned that one of

App.27a

the witnesses was paid. Yes, the witness was paid $25 to take a few minutes or an hour or two of her time, whatever it was. Again, the case law provides that there's nothing wrong with this, Judge. In fact, that's what occurred. It was a neighbor in the building and that's how that came about. So, I don't think that that—that in any way colors the testimony of this witness as to the due execution particularly since all the witnesses' testimony . . .

[. . .]

MR. MESSINA: I just have one other point to address on counsel's points. He referred to the deposition, sorry, the statement of the broker named Jeffrey Kern. That statement. was not. admittance to form. It's not a testimonial statement. It was not sworn to. Mr. Kern has not authenticated-the statement. It was not submitted along with a business record certificate, and, without it, we submit that statement is inadmissible. **Even if the Court were to rely on it, if you read the statement Sidney Fields actually states that he can read with a magnifying glass. So, to the extent the Court wishes to rely on that, we ask the Court to also consider that fact.**

In addition to the fact that the statement may say legally blind, which is a far cry from being actually blind. An actually blind person may still execute a will. Counsel indicated or alluded to—sorry, excuse me—alleged that Attorney Curtin did not read the will to the decedent. Testimony is the exact opposite of that fact. Mr. Curtin testified extensively that he sat side-by-side of

App.28a

the decedent, reviewed provisions of the will, including the provisions the decedent himself drafted and some boilerplate provisions. The parts that he couldn't read, Curtin read with him, and he'd seen him also use his magnifying glass with respect to the dispositive provisions of the will. Mr. Curtin testified the decedent knew everything that was in that will.

MR. HAAS: Just one more point and then I'll allow counsel to respond. With respect to the decedent's eyesight, Judge, his—there's nothing in the record where the objectant provides any indication as to any specific demission of the decedent's eyesight. There's—

THE COURT: But the client does not dispute that the decedent did not have perfect vision.

MR. HAAS: We do not dispute that, Judge, but that doesn't mean that he couldn't fully and completely read and compare and execute his will. And the objectant hasn't presented anything in any viable form to show otherwise.

MR. MESSINA: One final point, your Honor? If I may—

THE COURT: No. Mr. Chen?

MR. CHEN: Yes. Your Honor, as far as my trying to pull a fast one on them in terms of submitting a report that they'd never seen; I'm not understanding that argument. I simply went back to my records as to the report that I have that—and I say to the Court I'll make it very easy. The one that I submitted previously on the previous initial Motion by Mr. Curtin to dismiss our case, that's

App.29a

the one that I was referring to because Mr. Haas doesn't mention that he makes a great deal in his responsive papers about how he's never heard of my . . .

[. . .]

. . . if you go back to the testimony of the witnesses, you'll find Jill Curtin, by the way is the wife of the attorney draftsman, she's one of the witnesses. The other one is the paid witness. The attorney draftsman, oh, he was great. He walked in no problem he could see. One witness, Jill Curtin, said yeah, I don't really remember if he used a magnifying glass or not.

THE COURT: Mr. Chen, I think you made that point.

MR. CHEN: I made that point.

THE COURT: I (inaudible) on the papers.

MR. CHEN: Thank you. Thank you, your Honor.

THE COURT: It seems to me that one of your clients wants to talk to you. So, do you want to take a moment to talk to them?

MR. CHEN: I will say this, your Honor, I don't know (inaudible) I see you have a full room.

THE COURT: Correct.

MR. CHEN: If I—I know what's going to happen so, I'm just going to say ahead of time, if you allow me to talk to one of my clients, will you allow me to say one more sentence or two after I come back because if you don't I'm just going to (inaudible).

THE COURT: I'll give you one second to do that.

MR. CHEN: Thank you.

App.30a

THE COURT: You can come back in and what is not going to be, I'm not going to be—give you a lot of time to do that.

MR. CHEN: I'm not looking for that, your Honor. Thank you.

THE COURT: Okay.

MR. CHEN: Thank you.

(PAUSE 10:51:13 TO 10:52:53.)

THE COURT: Mr. Chen, anything that you would like to add after speaking with your clients?

MR. CHEN: Yes. Just two other points, your Honor. The documents of Mr. Kern the broke where the decedent stated that he was not able to read documents two days before the will signing were provided in discovery. They were—I obtained them by subpoena that's all on that and they're submitted in opposition.

I did have a conversation with one of my client's relatives and they are asking me to stress to the Court that the question of whether or not the decedent knew what he was signing is an issue before the Court that the will was not read out loud. From our standpoint and our documentation and our arguments, he did not know what he was signing and that is because the will was not read out loud. Even petitioner's own statements and it's in the record that she—that the draftsman attorney claimed was made by the decedent as to distribution under this particular will being proffered, don't match the actual will conditions and so, again, there' s a question of credibility and that credibility affects whether or not the decedent

App.31a

knew the terms of what he was signing, what he actually signed, and what condition—I have to say I don' t have the argument of testamentary capacity because your Honor is using documents of that were produced in discovery concerning, and by the way they' re on the same level as the Jeffrey Kern document, because those are not sworn either. Where he went to the hospital the next day and the doctor made observations, but if you go further into the documentation, you'll see that there is some discrepancy even as to even what that doctor initially, at the emergency room, initially wrote down.

In any event, that was why the client asked me to step outside because she wanted me to stress that he did not know what he was signing and on a more far reaching theory, that in reality what he—what he allegedly signed, the will that's being proffered, is not and did not contain the terms that he wanted.

THE COURT: Okay. I am going to determine this Motion today, but only to extent of indicating that I conclude from all the proof submitted by proponents in support of this Motion for Summary Determination that proponent made a prima facie showing of entitlement to judgment as a matter of law concerning the capacity of the decedent towards the instrument, the execution of the instrument by the decedent in compliance with statutory requirements and that the instrument was an actual will and not the product of undue influence, fraud or duress.

And, in opposition, objectant has failed to demonstrate through admissible evidence the existence

App.32a

of a material question of fact required in a trial as to any of the objections. So, proponent's Motion for Summary Determination the probate proceeding is going to be granted and the objections to probate are dismissed.

I will issue a decision explaining my reasoning and that decision will be mailed to both sides. Thank you.

MR. HAAS: Thank you very much, Judge.

MR. CHEN: Thank you, your Honor. We (inaudible). Thank you.

(THE PROCEEDINGS ENDED AT 10:57:00.)

[. . .]

App.33a

APPENDIX B
DOCTOR'S NOTE & TRANSCRIPTS
OF TELEPHONE RECORDINGS FROM VANGUARD

App.34a

SUBPOENA DUCES TECUM TO DR. JANET SEARLE (JUNE 5 AND JUNE 20, 2017)

SURROGATE'S COURT OF THE STATE OF NEW YORK, COUNTY OF NEW YORK

Probate Proceeding,
Will of SIDNEY H. FIELDS

Deceased.

THE PEOPLE OF THE STATE OF NEW YORK

File No. 2016-111

Before: The Honorable Rita MELLA,
Surrogate Court Judge

To: Dr. Janet Searle
17 East 102rd Street
New York, New York 10029

GREETTNG:

WE COMMAND YOU, THAT all business and excuses being laid aside, you and each of you produce to the law fam of <u>Novick and Associates, P.C.</u>, with offices located at <u>202 East Main Street, Suite 208, Huntington, New York 11743</u>, on <u>June 30, 2017 at 2:00 p.m.</u> and at any recessed or adjourned date and that you produce at the time and place aforesaid:

> Any and all records, including, but not limited to, progress notes, Health Care Proxies,

App.35a

Powers of Attorney that concern, refer or relate to the decedent, Sydney H. Fields, Social Security No. 103-10-1334, having an address at 372 Central Park West, Apt 20P, New York, New York 10025, for the period October 6, 2011 thorough and including November 10, 2015.

The reason why discovery is sought is that, upon information and belief, you have knowledge and are in possession of information and documents material and relevant to the prosecution of the objections to probate of the purported Last Will and Testament of Sydney H. Fields dated October 6, 2014, the Decedent's estate plan, the his health care and personal finances.

WE FURTHER COMMAND YOU to deliver to Novick & Associates, P.C. at the time of your production a certification in the form prescribed by CPLR § 3122-a, sworn in the form of an affidavit and subscribed by the custodian or other qualified witness charged with the responsibility of maintaining the records as annexed hereto.

Failure to comply with this subpoena is punishable as contempt of Court and shall make you liable to the person on whose behalf this subpoena was issued for a penalty not to exceed one hundred and fifty dollars ($150.00) and all damages sustained by reason of your failure to comply.

WITNESS, Hon. Rita Mella, Surrogate's Court of the State of New York, New York County, 31 Chambers Street, New York, N.Y. 10007 this 5th day of June, 2017.

App.36a

/s/ Albert V. Messina Jr., Esq.
Novick & Associates, P.C.
Trial Counsel for
Petitioner, Diana Palmeri
202 East Main Street, Suite 208
Huntington, NY 11743
(631) 547-0300

Dated: June 5, 2017
      Huntington, New York.

App.37a

EYE DOCTOR'S RESPONSE TO SUBPOENA

SURROGATE'S COURT OF THE STATE OF
NEW YORK, COUNTY OF NEW YORK

Probate Proceeding,
Will of SIDNEY H. FIELDS

Deceased.

File No. 2016-111

Notice of Subpoena Duces Tecum

State of NY
County of NY

Janet Serle, MD, being duly sworn, is a Custodian of Records for Dr. Janet Searle. In accordance with CPLR § 3122-a, the following is true under the penalties of perjury concerning our files regarding Sydney H. Fields:

1. The affiant is dully authorized custodian or other qualified witness and has authority to make the certification;

2. To the best of the affiant's knowledge, after reasonable inquiry, the records or copies thereof are accurate versions of the documents described in the attached subpoena duces tecum that are in the possession, custody, or control of the person receiving the subpoena duces tecum;

App.38a

3. To the best of the affiant's knowledge, after reasonable inquiry, the records or copies produced represent all the documents described in the attached subpoena duces tecum, or if they do not represent a complete set of the documents requested, an explanation of which documents are missing and a reason for their absence is provided; and

4. The records or copies produced were made by the personnel or staff or the business, or persons acting under their control, in the regular course of business, at the time of the act, transaction, occurrence or event recorded therein, or with a reasonable time thereafter, and that it was the regular course of business to make such records.

By: /s/ Janet Serle, MD
Prof. of Ophthalmology

Sworn to before me this 20th day of June, 2017

/s/ Christian A. Mota Velez
Notary Public-State of New York
No. 01MO6356185
Qualified in New York County
My Commission Expires Mar 27, 2021

App.39a

Slit Lamp and Fundus Exam

- External Exam

External	Right	Left
	p, Ptosis	p, Ptosis

- Slit Lamp Exam

	Right	Left
Lids/Lashes	1+ Ptosis, 1+ Blepharitis	1+ Ptosis, 1+ Blepharitis
Conjuctiva/ Sctera	1+ Conjunctival Injection	1+ Conjunctival Injection

[. . .]

App.40a

I Janet Serie MD attest that Hannah Palmer is acting in a scribe capacity, has observed my performance of the services and has documented them in accordance with my direction.

Revision History

Date Reviewed 6/7/2013

Problem List	Priority
Low back pain (Chronic)	High
Codes	**Noted Resolved**
D-10-CM:M54.5　ICD-90CM: 724.2	10/21/2014-Present　9/3/2014-Present
Problem List	**Priority**
Pseudoexfollation glaucoma	High
Codes	**Noted Resolved**
ICD-10-CM: H40.1490　ICD-9-CM: 365.52, 365.70	9/3/2014-Present
Problem List	**Priority**
Peripheral retinal degeneration	High
Codes	**Noted Resolved**
ICD-10-CM: H35.40　ICD-9-CM: 362.60	11/7/2013-Present

App.41a

Ophthalmology Record of Sydney Fields

Birth History: None
Custom History: None
Abuse and Neglect: None

History Reviewed

Date Reviewed:
    Last Reviewed by SERLE, JANET on 7/23/2015

Base Eye Exam

Visual Acuity (Snellen-Linear)

Dist SC	Right	Left
	CF at 3'	LP

Tonometry (Applanation, 12:02 PM)

Pressure	Right	Left
	14	28

Pupils

Dark	Right	Left
	3	3

Visual Fields

Result	Right	Left
		Full

Extraocular Movement

Result	Right	Left
	Full	Full

App.42a

Neuro/Psych
>Oriented x3: Yes
>Mood/Affect: Normal

Edited by: Shanel Shropshire, Janet B. Serie, MD

==========================

Last Reviewed by SERLE, JANET on 09/03/2014

Base eye exam

Visual Acuity(Snellen-Linear)

	Right	Left
Dist sc	CF at 3'	LP
Dis tph sc	NI	

App.43a

Problem List	Priority
Blind in both eyes	*Low*
Codes	Noted Resolved
ICD-10-CM: H54.0 *ICD-9-CM: 369.00*	*12/5/2014-Present*
Problem List	Priority
Frail elderly	Low
Codes	Noted Resolved
ICD-10-CM: R54 ICD-9-CM: 797	12/5/2014-Present
Problem List	Priority
CAD (coronary artery disease) (Chronic)	Low
Codes	Noted Resolved
ICD-10-CM: 125.10 ICD-9-CM: 414.00	10/21/2014-Present
Problem List	Priority
Weakness	Low
Codes	Noted Resolved
ICD-10-CM: R53.1 ICD-9-CM: 780.79	10/20/2014-Present
Problem List	Priority
PVD (peripheral vascular disease)	Low
Codes	Noted Resolved
ICD-10-CM: 173.9 ICD-9-CM: 443.9	10/8/2014-Present

App.44a

Problem List	Priority
Legally Blind	*Low*
Codes	Noted Resolved
ICD-10-CM: H54.8 ICD-9-CM: 369.4	9/3/2014-Present
Problem List	Priority
Ptosis	Low
Codes	Noted Resolved
ICD-10-CM: H02.409 ICD-9-CM: 374.30	4/23/2014-Present
Problem List	Priority
BPH with obstruction/lower urinary tract symptoms	Low
Codes	Noted Resolved
ICD-10-CM: N40.1, N13.8 ICD-9-CM: 600.01, 599.69	12/20/2013-Present
Problem List	Priority
MGD (Meibomian gland disease)	Low
Codes	Noted Resolved
ICD-10-CM: H01.009 ICD-9-CM: 373.00	11/7/2013-Present
Problem List	Priority
Cardiac pacemaker in altu	Low
Codes	Noted Resolved
ICD-10-CM: Z95.0 ICD-9-CM: V45.01	6/23/2013-Present

App.45a

Overview signed 6/23/2013 2:10 PM by Mary Courtney, NP. 11.2.11 SJM: SC PPM	
Problem List	**Priority**
Pseudophakia	Low
Codes	**Noted Resolved**
ICD-10-CM: Z96.1 ICD-9-CM: V43.1	4/25/2013-Present
Problem List	**Priority**
Pseudoexfollation glaucoma	Low
Codes	**Noted Resolved**
	4/1/2013-Present

App.46a

OBJECTANT'S SUBPOENA TO VANGUARD (FEBRUARY 21, 2017)

SURROGATE'S COURT OF THE STATE OF
NEW YORK, COUNTY OF NEW YORK

In the Matter of the

Last Will and Testament of
SIDNEY H. FIELDS

Deceased.

File No. 2016-111

STATE OF NEW YORK TO:

Jeffrey A. Kern
C/O Vanguard Group, Inc.
ATTN: Legal Department-M35
400 Devon Park Drive
Wayne, Pennsylvania 19087

WE COMMAND YOU to appear at <u>Veritext Legal Solutions, 1801 Market Street, Suite 1800, Philadelphia, Pennsylvania 19103 at 10.00 AM on March 24, 2017</u> to testify at a deposition to be taken in this action as to your knowledge and information related to the Decedent Sydney H. Fields.

You must also bring with you to the deposition any and all relevant and material papers, writings, correspondence and/or other documents in existence

App.47a

in connection with this matter, including complete and accurate copies of the following:

1. Any and all records of telephone conversations, email communications, or other correspondence, with SYDNEY H. FIELDS regarding any of his accounts with Vanguard for the period of 10/6/2011 to 11/10/2015; and

2. Any and all records of telephone conversations, email communications, or other correspondence, with DIANA PALMERI regarding any of SYDNEY H. FIELDS' accounts with Vanguard for the period of 10/6/2011 to 11/10/2015.

We represent the Objectant Richard Fields, who has commenced an action with regard to the Estate of Sydney H. Fields, in the above-entitled case. Diana Palmeri is the executor of the estate and had agent authorization on Sydney H. Fields' accounts. Disclosure is being sought from you because, upon information and belief, you possess relevant material which is necessary for the litigation of this action, and which is not reasonably available from any of the parties. Statutory compensation will be provided for the production of records requested herein.

If you are notified that a motion to quash the subpoena has been filed, the subpoenaed evidence shall not be produced or released until ordered to do so by the court or the release is consented to by all parties to the action.

Failure to comply with the command of this subpoena without reasonable excuse is punishable as a contempt of Court may subject you to the penalties provided by the New York Civil Practice Law and Rules.

App.48a

/s/ Richard Alan Chen, Esq.
Attorney for Objectant,
Richard Fields
41-60 Main Street, Ste. 203
Flushing, NY 11355
Tel: (718) 886-8181

Flushing, New York
Dated: 2/21/2017

App.49a

VANGUARD RESPONSE TO SUBPOENA (MARCH 17, 2017)

Via FedEx

Richard Alan Chen, Esquire
Law Offices of Richard Alan Chen, Esquire
41-60 Main Street, Suite 203
Flushing, NY 11355

RE: In the Matter of the Last Will and Testament of Sydney H. Fields
File No. 2016-111

Dear Mr. Chen:

On behalf of The Vanguard Group, Inc. ("Vanguard"), I am responding to the February 21, 2017 subpoena duces tecum regarding the above-captioned matter. Gina Kim, Esq., of your office provide Vanguard until March 21, 2017 to respond to the subpoena.

Vanguard objects to the subpoena (i) to the extent that the language used in the subpoena is vague and ambiguous; (ii) to the extent that it is overly broad or the production of documents in response to the subpoena would be unduly burdensome; (iii) to the extent that it seeks the production of documents that are irrelevant and not reasonably calculated to lead to the discovery of admissible evidence; and (iv) to the extent that it requests the production of documents that are protected from disclosure by the attorney-client privilege, the attorney work product doctrine, and/or any other applicable privilege or exemption.

Subject to and without waiver of the foregoing objections, Vanguard is enclosing on a USB flash drive, the following responsive documents, Bates labeled,

App.50a

VGI-1017833-000001 through VGI-1017833-000963, and telephone call recordings:

Sydney H. Fields-Individual Account 1
- 10/31/2011 through 12/31/2011 statements, sufficient to show monetary account activity for 10/6/2011 through 12/31/2011
- 1/1/2012-11/30/2015 statements, sufficient to show monetary account activity for 1/1/2012 through 11/10/2015
- Purchase check copies
- Checkwriting redemption checks
- 4-30-2015 correspondence from Sydney Fields plus Agent Authorization (SSN and DOB for Diana Palmeri have been redacted)
- Agent Authorization (Teresa Fields)

Sydney H. Fields-Individual Account 2 and Individual Account 3
- Monetary Transcripts, sufficient to show monetary account activity from inception through close (separated by Vanguard fund code)
- 5-31-2015 through 11-30-2015 statements (fund code 531 only, individual account 3)
- Checkwriting redemption checks
- CWR form
- Change of Ownership Forms for Transfers due to death, Account Registration Form, Death Certificate, Form W-9 from

App.51a

**Theresa M. Fields & Sydney H. Fields—
Jt. Ten. WROS***

- 10/31/2011 through 12/31/2011 statements, sufficient to show monetary account activity for 10/6/2011 through 12/31/2011
- 1/1/2012-12/31/2014 statements, sufficient to show monetary account activity for 1/1/2012 through 12/31/2014

Sydney H. Fields

- 3-25-2014 correspondence from Jeffrey A Kern
- Agent Authorization (Diana Palmeri)
- Cost Basis Method Election Form

Emails

- Emails from Jeffrey Kern to Diana Palmeri
- Emails from Diana Palmeri to Jeffrey Kern

The above email search was conducted for 10-6-2011—11-10-2015, as limited by Gina Kim, Esq., of your office on March 8, 2017.

Telephone call recordings

- All located telephone call recordings between Sydney Fields and Jeffrey Kern for 10-1-2013—10-10-2015, as limited by Gina Kim, Esq., of your office on March 8, 2017.
- All located telephone call recordings between Diana Palmeri and Jeffrey Kern for 10-1-2013—most recent (as of 3-14-2017), as limited by Gina Kim, Esq., of your office on March 8, 2017. Certain personal information has been scrubbed

App.52a

from these calls to protect personal security information for account holder.

The USB flash drive is password protected, on March 8, 2017, I provided Gina Kim, Esq., of your office with the password

If you have any questions concerning this matter, please contact me at 610-669-9374.

Sincerely

/s/ Miles Gilpin
Legal Analyst
Legal Department

Enclosures

cc: Diana Palmeri (letter only, via first-class mail}

App.53a

OBJECTANT FORWARDING VANGUARD'S USB TO PETITIONER (MARCH 24, 2016)

LAW OFFICES OFFICES OF RICHARD ALAN CHEN, ESQ.
41-60 Main Street, Suite 203
Flushing, NY 11355
(718) 886-8181 (Tel.)/(718) 886-8011 (Fax)
raclawoffice3@gmail.com

Novick & Associates, P.C.
202 East Main Street
Huntington, New York 11743
Attn: Albert V. Messina, Jr.

    Re: Estate of Sydney Fields, Deceased/
         File No. 2016-111

Dear Mr. Messina:

Attached please find, for service upon you, **VANGUARD PRODUCTION IN RESPONSE TO SUBPOENA**, all documents included on attached USB flash drive.

Please be guided accordingly. Thank you.

                    Very truly yours,

                    /s/ Richard Alan Chen, Esq.

App.54a

DECEDENT'S AGENT AUTHORITY TO TERESA'S VANGUARD ACCOUNT (MARCH 25, 2014)

Sydney H. Fields
372 Central Park W Apt 20P
New York, NY 10025-8213

Dear Mr. Fields:

This letter confirms that you are listed as having agent authority on Teresa M. Fields' Vanguard® individual accounts #88034756999 and #09881518660, as of March 24, 2014.

If you have any questions, please call me at 866-414-2325, on business days from 8 a.m. to 10 p.m. or on Saturdays from 9 a.m. to 4 p.m., Eastern time. If I'm unavailable, you can speak with another representative, or you can leave me a voice mail and I will return your call.

Sincerely,

/s/ Jeffrey A. Kern
Registered Representative
52620090

App.55a

VANGUARD TELEPHONE TRANSCRIPT (OCTOBER 1, 2014)

Phone Conversation between Jeffrey Kern & Sydney Fields [October 1, 2014, Transcript]

(Phone ringing and Mr. Fields answers.)

MR. FIELDS: Hello.

MR. KERN: Hello, Mr. Fields?

MR. FIELDS: Yes.

MR. KERN: Hi, this is Jeffrey Kern of Vanguard recorded line, how are you?

MR. FIELDS: Okay.

MR. KERN: Good, good, do you have a couple of minutes?

MR. FIELDS: Certainly.

MR. KERN: Okay, and if you don't mind if you could provide your password for me.

MR. FIELDS: Miss, M-I-S-S.

MR. KERN: Okay, great, thank you so much. I know you've been in contact with colleague Andrew regarding the passing of your wife Theresa.

MR. FIELDS: Right.

MR. KERN: Right, I'm terribly sorry to hear about that.

MR. FIELDS: Uh, you know, I appreciate that.

MR. KERN: Yeah.

MR. FIELDS: Uh.

App.56a

MR. KERN: I also understand that you were having some difficulty with the, the forms that Andrew had sent out to you.

MR. FIELDS: Yes, because I can't read, you know, I'm, I'm, I'm legally blind, although I—that's not like being actually blind, but—

MR. KERN: Right, I know I called you—

MR. FIELDS: I can't read, I can't read, I can't read any type, you know, and, and that's why I can't handle those pages, you know, I, I have, I have the Death Certificate of Theresa Fields and I can mail you in the Death Certificate, but I, I can't fill out those, those papers that were mailed to me.

MR. KERN: Okay, can you see them at all to read them or even if you—

MR. FIELDS: I, I, I, I, I can't, I can't read them, no, I can't read.

MR. KERN: Okay.

MR. FIELDS: I mean, with my magnifying glass I can read large print, but I can't read anything that's—that's on, that's on papers.

MR. KERN: Okay.

MR. FIELDS: I was wondering if I could come in and then and like I did with Chase Bank and I sat at the desk and the girl asked me questions and I answered them and that's how I finally transferred my wife's bank accounts, because I gave her the Death Certificate.

MR. KERN: Sure, okay. What I'd like to do, because as far as you coming down to Malvern, I think we

App.57a

might even be able to do better than that and possibly come up and see you, which I think might be a little easier.

MR. FIELDS: Oh that would be great, that would be wonderful, I appreciate that.

MR. KERN: Okay, I do need to just look into a few things here first just before we can nail down a date, but, but I, once I do that, then I'll be back in touch with you and then hopefully we can schedule a time that works for both of us, does that sound okay?

MR. FIELDS: That sounds fine.

MR. KERN: Okay, all right, well I've been in touch with Andrew here at Vanguard, so we're both on the same page here, let me do some work on my end and I'll be in back, I'll be back in touch with you, just looking, let's see, it's about 4 o'clock, so I'll be in touch with you tomorrow or Friday, so definitely before the week is out.

MR. FIELDS: Okay, but—

MR. KERN: Okay.

MR. FIELDS: Friday I have an appointment with an Attorney from 2 o'clock on, so I won't be available after 2 o'clock on Friday, but, but up until 2 o'clock I'll be available and I'll be available all day tomorrow.

MR. KERN: All right, then I shoot for, okay, then either tomorrow or earlier in the day on Friday if it goes that far.

MR. FIELDS: That's very good.

App.58a

MR. KERN: All right, well thank you so much for your time I'll be back in touch, we'll, we'll go from there.

MR. FIELDS: Okay, thank you, I'll wait for your call.

MR. KERN: Sounds good, all right.

MR. FIELDS: Goodbye.

MR. KERN: Take care, bye now.

[END OF PHONE CONVERSATION]

App.59a

VANGUARD TELEPHONE TRANSCRIPTS —RELEVANT EXCERPTS

Phone Conversation between Jeffrey Kern & Sydney Fields [October 3, 2014, Transcript]

[. . .]

MR. FIELDS: Yes.

MR. KERN: Do you believe that your Attorney would be able to help you out with these forms?

MR. FIELDS: No, no, he knows nothing about the forms.

MR. KERN: Okay.

MR. FIELDS: I'm not discussing any forms with him.

MR. KERN: Yeah.

MR. FIELDS: I'm discussing something altogether different.

MR. KERN: Okay, okay, that was just a question that had come up if the Attorney could, could assist you with this.

MR. FIELDS: No, no. No, I'm no, no, he has—he doesn't know anything about these forms, so I didn't mention anything to him.

MR. KERN: Okay. Is there anybody else that you would trust to help you with the forms?

MR. FIELDS: What?

MR. KERN: Is there anybody else that you would trust to help you with the forms that could read them to you?

App.60a

MR. FIELDS: Well I, I mean, I have a niece that, that's, that helps me read a letter sometimes, I mean, she, what could she do with, I thought, I thought you were going to make arrangements there to see me about the forms?

MR. KERN: Well, and I'm still working on that, as well, but I just wanted to see if it, if there was a convenient way, if there's somebody else that could read them to you and we could do a, a conference call or something to that effect, that's what I was just getting—

MR. FIELDS: I mean, I mean, I have a niece there that she knows, knows nothing, nothing about, about, about, about the Law or anything, I mean, she knows how to, she's an educated person, but I don't know whether she can interpret the forms.

MR. KERN: Okay, so, again, I just wanted to see if that was, my group here was asking if there was somebody that you trust to read the forms to you and we could do a conference call to answer any question.

MR. FIELDS: I, I haven't, I haven't, I haven't, I haven't shown any of the forms to her and I mentioned that I got the letters from you and that I can't handle it.

MR. KERN: Okay.

MR. FIELDS: But I haven't, I haven't, I haven't shown her the, I haven't, I haven't given her . . .

[. . .]

App.61a

Phone Conversation between Jeffrey Kern & Sydney Fields [March 26, 2015, Transcript]

[. . .]

MR. FIELDS: Yes.

MR. KERN: So at Vanguard when we add an Agent it's done at the account level, not at the fund level. So if you name an Agent it would be for all the funds in that account.

MR. FIELDS: Well, well, I mean, that puts me at a disadvantage, I mean, she had, she has access to all of my accounts and I could be dispossessed if I have an argument with her or anything. I want to limit her to one account, is there anyway that can be done?

MR. KERN: Uh.

MR. FIELDS: I mean, can I open up a, a, can I shift that account to, to another title?

MR. KERN: Well, you could open up, you could move assets into a new fund, you know, in its own account with a new account number, so we could do that and then you would name her just on the one account, so it would still be by the account number, but if there's only one fund in that account—

MR. FIELDS: Yeah.

MR. KERN: Then that's the only one she would have authority over. So is it that you wanted her to have access to that limited term tax exempt?

MR. FIELDS: Yes.

MR. KERN: So for check writing, things like that?

App.62a

MR. FIELDS: Yeah, yeah, right, for check, for bank bills, right.

MR. KERN: Okay, so you would want to name her as a full Agent so she can do all that for you.

MR. FIELDS: Right.

MR. KERN: But, yeah, that would mean shifting all this over into a new account which, I mean, we can do that, we—

MR. FIELDS: Okay, so that's okay with me.

MR. KERN: All right, so then, let me take a quick look here, yep, do you have any outstanding checks right now?

MR. FIELDS: I mean, I, I, I, I don't look at the checks, I, I mean, I only issue, I only issue one check a month on that account and that's the one I want her to issue so the last, last check we issued I think was in March, did that check clear?

MR. KERN: In March, March 12th, there was a payment for American Express?

MR. FIELDS: Yes.

MR. KERN: Okay.

MR. FIELDS: As long as that, there's no other check.

[. . .]

Phone Conversation between Jeffrey Kern & Sydney Fields [March 26, 2015, Transcript]

[. . .]

. . . you check off saying you're adding one or more Agents, then you put the name of the Agent, where you put your name.

App.63a

MS. PALMERI : Um hum.

MR. KERN: And then below that you can even just write in, you know, Full Agent only on, and then put the fund and account number.

MS. PALMERI : Only on fund name and account number.

MR. KERN: Right.

MS. PALMERI : Okay.

MR. KERN: So I would, I would put it there as well as that signed letter of instruction just clarifying what, what's going on, that you're remaining as Limited Agent, but you're just being named as a Full Agent for this one specific fund.

MS. PALMERI : Okay, but you check Full Agent for every, like it wouldn't, like if you didn't have a letter in, it would be Full Agent for everything, but then include the letter.

MR. KERN: Correct.

MS. PALMERI : Okay, okay.

MR. KERN: Yeah, because the form itself it really, it is a Durable Power of Attorney Document and it's not by fund, it's by registration, so it does . . .

[. . .]

App.64a

LETTER FROM AUTHORIZATION SYDNEY FIELDS TO JEFFREY KERN

To the attention of:

    Jeffrey Kern
    Client Relationship Administrator
    Vanguard Flagship Services
    E-mail: jeffrey_kern@fs.vanguard.com
    Phone: 866-414-2325

Dear Mr. Kern,

I, Sydney H. Fields, am requesting that, even though on my agent authorization form I am checking "All individually owned nonretirement accounts" be given full authority to Diana Palmeri, with this letter I am requesting that Diana Palmeri, my niece, be given full authority on only the following fund (with check writing ability):

- Fund Name: Vanguard Limited-Term Tax-Exempt Fund Admiral Shares
- Acct # 0531-00971376481

She is to retain limited authority on all other funds.

Thank you for your help with this matter.

Sincerely

/s/ Sydney H. Fields

App.65a

APPENDIX C
PERJURY ABOUT SYDNEY'S VISION

App.66a

TESTIMONY OF DIANA PALMIERI

[Diana Palmieri Testimony–Transcript, p.109]

A. He would read his documents with a magnifying glass.

Q. But he could read?

A. Yes.

Q. You observed him reading documents?

A. I observed him reading, yes.

Q. Did he have any problems with hearing in August of 2014?

A. He had hearing aids.

Q. What about in September, was his condition the same as August of 2014?

A. I think so.

Q. What about October of 2014, specifically up to and including October 6th, what was his condition with sight, hearing and being able to physically sign?

A. Seemed the same to me. He used the magnifying glass. He used hearing aids (indicating).

Q. In August of 2014, did you ever see him sign any documents, August of 2014?

A. August?

[. . .]

Exclusive of our court meetings.

App.67a

> What about Louis Fields, who would be, as far as I know, the grandson, Pia and Richard Fields' grandson.

A. I think he came to court once.

Q. You never met him before that?

A. I don't remember meeting him, no.

Q. What about an attorney by the name of Edward Curtin, have you ever spoken to him?

A. **I spoke to him at the will signing—the will signing—sorry, I did not say will signing. At the will reading, will reading.**

Q. You spoke to him at a will reading?

A. Yeah.

Q. When was that?

A. it was after Syd passed away.

Q. Was that the first time you spoke to Mr. Curtin?

A. From what I remember.

Q. When did Mr. Fields pass away?

A. November 10th, 2015.

> **I did not mean to say will signing. I did not meet him at any will signing.**

Q. You said will reading, is what I heard?

A. Yeah.

Q. is it correct to say that you did not meet Mr. Curtin prior to this will reading which must have taken place after November 10th—

A. Not before that.

App.68a

Q. And you never had any connection with him at all; no contact, no phone calls?

A. I don't remember. I don't think so.

Q. Do you recall if Mr. Curtin or his office ever called you prior to November 10th, 2015?

A. I don't think so.

Q. What about your husband, if you know, did he ever have any contact with Mr. Curtin?

[. . .]

. . . the will of Teresa Fields was produced by Diana Palmeri to you for filing with the court?

A. I believe that's the case.

Q. What about for the will that we are now objecting to, who produced the will to you?

A. Also Ms. Palmeri.

Q. So, it's correct to state that there was a reading of the will in your office?

A. What do you mean by a reading?

Q. Where the parties come to your office and you read the will and they hear—

A. No, that didn't happen. You mean like on television, no, that didn't happen.

Q. I can only think of a Saturday Night Live skit many years ago about reading a will and unfortunately I think it was Bill Murray who said kind of slurring as the attorney. But it was a comedy sketch. That's all I can think of so that never happened; is that correct?

A. There was no formal reading of . . .

App.69a

[. . .]

. . . cabinet.

Q. So the first time you saw it was when you unlocked the file cabinet and took the will out; is that correct?

A. The first time I saw the will was when I opened the file cabinet and looked around and the will was there.

Q. Now, let me look at the document. Thank you.

(Witness handing.)

Q. I'd like to ask you exactly, if you know, the relationships of these parties with Sydney.

For instance, Olga Palmeri, how often did Olga Palmeri see Sydney Fields when he was alive?

A. So the usual, like the holidays, when she visited my aunt. They used to do shopping trips together. I don't know if he was there or not. It was mostly to see my aunt.

Q. Where does Olga Palmeri live?

A. 80 Forest Avenue.

Q. In New Jersey?

A. Yes.

Q. What city?

A. In Paramus.

Q. How old is she now?

A. 80. 80.

Q. And that's your mother?

App.70a

A. My mother.

Q. So in 2014, she was 78; is that correct?

A. I guess so. I think she's 80. Yeah.

Q. **Did Olga Palmeri ever take any vacations with Sydney—**

A. **no**.

Q. —to your knowledge?

A. Not to my knowledge.

Q. Did you ever observe any other types of interaction between Olga and Sydney except at these holidays—family gatherings?

A. No.

Q. What about Victor Palmeri, Jr.? Where does he live?

A. He lives in Hawaii, and I actually haven't spoken to him since 2006, '5. Something like that he had a huge out-falling (sic) with my father and we haven't spoken.

Q. That would be Victor Palmeri—

A. Jr. Jr. and senior—I just recently started e-mailing him.

Q. Now, Victor Palmeri Jr. lives in Hawaii. Did he live in Hawaii in 2014?

A. I don't know. I think he did. I don't know.

Q. What was the relationship between Mr. Victor Palmeri Jr. and Sydney Fields?

A. I don't know. I wasn't speaking to him.

App.71a

Q. Did you ever observe Sydney and Victor together—

A. Nope.

Q. —on a trip or anything like that?

A. No.

Q. Since 2006, had you ever seen Victor at a family gathering that you testified happened a lot?

A. No. I haven't seen him since the fallout.

Q. But Victor Palmeri Jr. and Sydney Fields, you do know that they've met? They have met in the past?

MR. HAAS: Objection.

A. Have they met in the past?

Q. Yes.

A. **In the past, yeah, because years ago, for example— you know, when we were in high school, yeah.**

Q. What about Cynthia Palmeri, where does she live?

A. She lives in North Carolina.

Q. Now she's living in North Carolina?

A. Yes.

Q. On Exhibit 1 it says she lives at 80 Forest Avenue.

Was she living at 80 Forest Avenue, Paramus, New Jersey, at the time that this will was made on October 6th, 2014?

A. No.

Q. She was not?

App. 72a

A. No.

Q. She was living in North Carolina?

A. Yes.

Q. And she was in 2014; is that correct?

A. Yes.

Q. So the will is incorrect; she didn't live at 80 Forest Avenue at that time when the will was made?

A. She did not live there.

Q. What was the relationship between Cynthia Palmeri and Sydney Fields?

A. You know, she comes up twice a year. She has a child with severe disabilities, autism, so she has a very hard time bringing him on airplanes and things. So she comes when she can.

Q. Did you observe Cynthia at these family gatherings at Sydney's—or with Sydney?

A. When she was around, yeah.

[. . .]

App.73a

TESTIMONY OF SUZANNE MARIE LEHMAN

[Suzanne Marie Lehman Testimony–Transcript]

A. Yes.

Q. You did. Okay.

So I'm just going to read from the first paragraph—it's actually the second because the first one is one sentence.

Said testator—this is the last sentence of what would be the second paragraph. Said testator a t the time of making such subscription declared the instrument so subscribed to be his last will and testament.

Did that happen? Did Mr. Field say, yes, that's my will, and that's why you signed the affidavit?

A. **To tell you the truth, the process was never—I mean, Mr. Fields spoke and agreed, and I have a feeling that the process was either—happened as we were—as we were doing it as part of the process.**

Whether he spoke up, I don't remember that he did and he said it to me, but it was definitely being led by his lawyer.

Q. This is going to go back.

Again, present was Mr. Curtin, his wife, Jill Curtin, yourself and Mr. Fields?

A. (Indicating).

Q. There were no other parties in the room; is that correct?

App.74a

A. I do not remember there being anyone else.

Q. Even the aide that you described was not in the room; is that correct?

A. I don't remember exactly; because they came in, got him in and I think they left. I'm not really—I was not—I was not concerned with the aide. I was mainly concerned with Mr. Fields.

Q. Now, the affidavit goes on to say that, Each of the undersigned thereupon signed his or her name as a witness at the end of the will at the request of said testator and in his presence and sight and in the presence and sight of each other.

[. . .]

. . . you signed it on that day is because there's a date on the document?

MR. HAAS: I'll object.

You can answer the question.

A. It says 10/6/14. I'm assuming that that was—I mean—it's very—if you could make a clear question that doesn't have dates and all of that on it.

That's my signature. I was only there on that day. That would have been the only time I signed it. If—that would have been the time. It didn't happen before, it didn't happen after. It happened when we were doing the process.

Q. Did you see Sydney Fields sign this document?

A. I must have.

Q. **But sitting here today, do you recall watching him sign—**

App.75a

A. **I do not recall.**
Q. But there is a signature here that—
A. That is definitely mine.
Q. And there's another signature?

[. . .]

App. 76a

TESTIMONY OF JILL CURTIN

[Jill Curtin Testimony–Transcript]

A. Yes.

Q. —or do you recognize it as your last will and testament?

A. Yes.

Q. Did Mr. Curtin read the will a loud before Mr. Fields and yourself and the other witness signed?

A. No. We—no.

Q. Did you see Mr. Fields read the will? Did you see him read the will?

A. I have a memory of a magnifying glass. It's a black rectangle with a handle. But I'm not sure if that was Mr. Fields. I believe he might have, you know . . . .

Q. Did you hear Mr. Curtin read the will to Mr. Fields?

A. No.

I don't know—I did not know what was in the will.

Q. Did Mr. Curtin read the will to Sydney Fields out loud?

A. Not in my presence.

Did you read the will?

[. . .]

. . . glass, but I'm not sure if that was Mr. Fields.

App.77a

Q. When you say "magnifying glass," do you recall if he was using a magnifying glass?

A. He might have used it and then initialed and signed (indicating)

Q. But you're not sure?

A. I am not sure.

Q. Also, since you testified Mr. Curtin did not read—or you did not hear Mr. Curtin read the will out loud—

A. Yes.

Q. —did you see Mr. Fields read the will, with or without the magnifying glass?

A. Well, I have this little memory of him with the magnifying glass, but . . . .

Q. Sitting here today, do you know any reason for why Mr. Fields would be using a magnifying glass to read his will?

A. I don't know what the reason—I don't know of any reason.

Q. Was there any mention at the . . . .

[. . .]

TESTIMONY OF E. CURTIN

[E. Curtin Testimony–Transcript]

. . . the line even though it is quite legible; it is correct that you said this in your affidavit, right?

A. That is correct, I said it and I meant it.

Q. Can you tell me how you discerned that Mr. Fields suffered from a serious vision impairment on October 6, 2014?

A. He stated that had he difficulty seeing. He had a magnifying glass that he utilized to see what he needed to see. He spoke of having to have eyedrops administered to him, which he hated. And he was not happy about his vision. He was—you know, he didn't like the fact that he had that.

Q. Did he say to you on October 6, 2014 that he would not be able to read his own will?

A. I think there was a combination of that. We sat side by side on the final version of the will and in part he was using his magnifying glass to read sections and part I would read to him, perhaps more of the boilerplate. I know he was focused on the certain boilerplate that he was quite familiar with, since this was our third will, one of which in fact in 2006 he had written himself, so he was conversed with that boilerplate part of the will, but that we both focused on and reading the who was getting what and who wasn't getting what, and those he was particularly interested in. And in those cases, I think he also used his magnifying glass to ascertain that what I was saying was there, was there.

App.79a

Q. Is it correct to state that Sydney Fields did not read himself his entire will?

A. He was there with a magnifying glass. We looked at every page. **Whether he—I wasn't inside his mind to know whether he actually read every single word.**

Q. Did Mr. Fields, while looking a t the will, say to you I'm sorry, I can't read any particular section of the will?

A. No.

Q. Do you recall what section of the will you read to him, as you sit here today?

[. . .]

. . . he made those statements?

A. He made—he subsequently made statements when we did the actual execution of the will with the witnesses present, that he declared it to be his last will and testament.

Q. So, when you say prior to his signing the will, is it correct to state that what you mean by that is, not just prior to his signing the will with the witnesses present but this took place at another time?

A. I don't understand your question.

Q. You say in your affirmation prior to signing his will I read the entire text thereof to Mr. Fields and he concurred it accurately reflected his testamentary wishes?

A. That's right.

Q. When did that happen?

A. Prior to the time we did the actual—we called the witnesses in to do the execution.

Q. So, the witnesses were not present when this took place; is that correct?

A. That's correct.

Q. Where were they?

A. I think Jill was sitting out in the outer room, call it the reception area, if you will, with the whatever, aid, Mr. Fields had come with. And Susan Lehman was in her apartment next door. She is our next door neighbor.

Q. How did you contact Susan Lehman to come and watch the execution of the will?

A. I told Jill that we were ready and would she kindly tap on her door and have Susan come over.

Q. And she did?

A. And she did.

Q. So, is it correct to state that this portion that you're saying hereof your affirmation, prior to signing his will I read the entire text thereof to Mr. Fields and he concurred that it accurately reflected his will. Just pertaining of the reading of the entire text, the witnesses were not present; isn't that correct?

A. That's correct.

[. . .]

. . . 2. in the previous superseded will, Mr. Fields had left the bulk of his estate to his wife, Teresa Fields, but when she died in September of 2014, Mr. Fields was compelled to have a new will

App.81a

drafted, wherein he provided for his residuary estate to be distributed amongst members of his deceased family whom he had come—

A. Deceased wife's family.

Q. Deceased wife's family, whom he had come to embraces as his own family. Specifically I'm going to zero in on questioning about Mr. Fields was compelled to have a new will drafted. You did write this, right, Mr. Curtin?

A. Those are my words.

Q. So, could you please just explain what you meant by Mr. Fields was compelled to have a new will drafted?

A. What I intended to convey there was that Mr. Fields on his own initiative determined that he needed to have a new will. It may have been in-artfully stated by me; the word compelled was not in any way. . . .

[. . .]

A. Prior to October 6, 2014.

Q. As you sit here today, do you recall if you gave these documents to Mr. Fields prior to his executing the actual will?

A. No.

Q. You did not give them to Mr. Fields?

A. I don't believe I gave them to Mr. Fields.

Q. Were these documents from your own files?

A. Yes.

Q. Where are the originals of these documents?

App.82a

A. I believe I gave them to Mr. Haas.

Q. But these are true and correct copies of the originals; is that correct?

A. True and correct, yes, they appear to be.

Q. Now, the final will has different distribution provisions than even Exhibit 8 or I believe either of these two markups; am I correct, either 12 or 13?

A. I'd have to look at the actual will.

Q. The actually will is here; that's our exhibit also.

A. The percentages of the residuary estate distribution and Article 4 of the actual will appear to be the same as the percentages set forth on Exhibit 13, Page 1946.

Q What about Exhibit 12?

A. Exhibit 12, again, this is a draft and the number of percentages next to Diana Palmeri looks like either a 40 percent or a 30 percent or the three written over the four or the four written over the three, neither of which matches the 35 that ended up being in the actual will itself.

Q. So, my question is as pertaining to your marked up copies, which would be drafts, right?

A. Uh-huh.

Q. of 13 and 12—yes, right?

A. Yes, well—

MR. HAAS: Can you just repeat that.

Q. as pertaining to 12 and 13—

A. Right.

App.83a

Q. —do you remember when you did these?

A. Well, both prior to October 6th and based on the percentages since the Exhibit 13—I would say Exhibit 13 I did after Exhibit 12.

Q. Do you recall how these changed?

A. Well, substantially.

MR. HAAS: I'll object.

You can answer it.

A. I mean, this—this, as I look a t it now, was done based on my notes in this one. When I say this, I mean Number Exhibit 12, because for example, I crossed out the provision here leaving the apartment to Teresa and in the Exhibit 13, that paragraph is out.

Q. Were those exhibits, 12 and 13, were those done after Exhibit 8 was given to you by Sydney Fields?

A. I believe so; I can't be certain.

Q. After the meeting of October 3rd, which you testified to, and prior to October 6th, did you have any further contact with Mr. Fields about changing the distributions?

A. There may have been a conversation, phone conversation. I don't recall.

Q. We have one last exhibit. This is Bates stamped 110, 000110, produced in discovery by your side. Is this dated September 30, 2014? Do you recognize that and is your signature on it?

A. Yes.

MR. CHEN: So, I would like to mark that as Exhibit 14.

App.84a

(Letter dated 9/30/14 was marked as Objectant's Exhibit 14, for identification, as of this date.)

Q. if you look at the letter, Mr. Curtin, you sent that letter on September 30, . . .

[. . .]

A. Yes.

Q. You testified Mr. Fields' hand was not shaking; is that correct?

A. That's correct.

Q. At the time he signed, did you instruct Mr. Fields as to where to sign as he was signing?

A. Well, with respect to the Pages 1 and 2, I asked him to initial the lower left-hand corner. And on Page 3 I asked him to sign above where his name was typed. At that time he asked me to put Xs there to help guide him and then he proceeded to sign.

Q. Is it correct to state that at the time that this will was executed, it was your practice as the supervising attorney to ask the testator to initial the pages that he was not signing on the will?

A. That is my practice.

Q. Okay, thank you. Were you present when the witnesses signed?

A. Yes.

Q. Was Mr. Fields present?

A. Yes.

Q. If you turn to Page 4 of the initialing process, excuse me for saying that, but there are initials that appear on the left-hand corner after the second paragraph, actually a t the second paragraph if you want to consider the first sentence a paragraph.

If you would, please explain to us how those initials came to pass, who they are and how that happened?

A. Okay. The—after the two witnesses had read and signed this affidavit and I had signed as the notary, Jill, my wife, was making, as is our practice, was making copies of the will and she pointed out to me in the process of making copies that this was—there was a blank in there and there was the date July 2006 and at that point I realized it was a carryover from a prior will, probably the prior will of Sid Fields off my word processing computer. And so in the presence of the witnesses and Mr. Fields, I made the correction on the—to reflect the actual date that it was, October 6, 2014, and initialed it.

Q. Did you request the witnesses to initial that change on their affidavit?

A. No.

Q. Why not?

A. I didn't think it was necessary.

Q. Is it correct to state that the witnesses never heard you read off to Mr. Fields the fourth paragraph of the will on Page 1 concerning the beneficiaries as to what their percentages would be, etcetera?

App.86a

A. The witnesses did not hear me read any of the provisions of the will at any time.

Q. If you know, were the witnesses observing Mr. Fields concerning the fourth paragraph in any way in his review of it?

MR. HAAS: I'll object. You can answer if you understand that.

A. Could you repeat the Question?

Q. I'll rephrase. Did Mr. Fields make any statements about the fourth paragraph while the witnesses were present and prior to signing?

A. Other than he declared the document to be his last will and testament, no.

Q. You'll notice on Page 3 of the will, that where the witnesses signed it's indicated that same, I'm paraphrasing, to be her last will and testament and We thereupon a t her request in her presence and the presence of each other have subscribed our names as attesting witnesses. That is what the document says, correct?

A. The document speaks for itself.

Q. Thank you. Can you explain how, obviously Mr. Fields was a man, how that reference was in there as her?

A. Yes, this was a carryover from a prior will that was used, a template if you will, and I agree it should say his but it says her.

Q. I'm going to refer to Objectant's 2. While the document speaks for itself, in that same clause for witnesses attesting to the will it also says her as well, with. . . .

App.87a

[. . .]

(. . . identification, as of this date.)

Q. Now, Mr. Curtin, you testified that you recognize this document. Can you tell me what it is, that's Exhibit 8?

MR. HAAS: Which document are you referring to?

A. Eight.

MR. HAAS: You testified that you recognized that before?

A. Yes. Just a short while ago.

Q. Yes.

A. This is a piece of paper with handwritten names and numbers next to those names that was given to me when I met with Mr. Sid Fields the first time for the purpose of preparing this 2014 will.

Q. Did Mr. Fields make out this sheet in front of you?

A. No.

Q. Can you tell me what he said, what you said, concerning when this was handed to you?

A. He said this is the way I want to have the—his estate, his residuary estate distributed.

Q. And, do you know if this document was made out by Mr. Fields?

A. I don't know for certain, but he is the only person that gave it to me, so.

Q. So, all you know is that he gave it to you, correct?

A. Yes.

App.88a

Q. What date did he give it to you?

A. That would have been—I think We met with him on October 3rd, so that's when he would have given it to me.

Q. You testified we. Who would be the we in that?

A. When did I say we?

Q. Just now, you said we met with him on October 3rd.

A. Can you read that back?

>(Whereupon, the record was read by the reporter.)

A. The we is me; it was the royal me.

Q. That's the law office of Edward Curtin met with him?

[. . .]

. . . intended to indicate that he was under any kind of duress, but that it was his own initiative to have a new will drafted because his wife had died.

Q. Did he ever tell you why he wanted to change his will from the previous will in effect, which was the 2006 will?

A. Yes, because the 2006 will left substantial portions of his estate, there was some kind of life estate, was left to his wife, his then living wife, Teresa. After she had died, she was no longer there to be a beneficiary and Mr. Fields decided to have a new will drafted.

Q. Now, on that same page as We go down to the bottom you write, what was not changed in the

App.89a

October 6, 2014 will was the following, Provision 5B, because my son, Richard Fields, hired a lawyer to sue me for money because I had to have him arrested and brought to court for harassment of me and my wife Teresa. I deliberately make no provision for him in this will and it is my intention that he receive no part of the estate. You wrote that, right, Mr. Curtin?

MR. MESSINA: Objection.

Did he write it in this affirmation or the original will?

Q. First in this affirmation.

A. I typed it in this affirmation.

Q. Did, Mr. Fields specifically reference this provision you're mentioning when he talked to you about changing his previous will and doing the new will that we are objecting to?

A. Yes, he wanted to be sure that this provision was left in the 2014 will as well as the provision relating to his son, Kenneth.

Q. It's correct to state that both of these provisions were in the 2006 will?

A. That's correct. Well, there is no provision referenced in this affidavit with respect to Kenneth, but there was another provision related to Kenneth in 2006 will, that was also incorporated into the 2014 will at Mr. Fields' express direction.

[. . .]

App.90a

RETURN OF DOCUMENTS TO RICHARD CHEN (AUGUST 24, 2018)

ATTORNEYS AT LAW
202 East Main Street
Huntington, New York 11743
Telephone (631) 547-0300
Facsimile (631) 547-0212

Donald Novick
John P. Graffeo
Michael J. Sullivan*
Kimberly A. Schechter
Albert V. Messina, Jr.
Alice Jakyung Choi*
Of Counsel:
    Kaitlyn A. Blanchard*

* Also Admitted in New Jersey

10 Rockefeller Plaza
New York, NY 10020
Telephone: (212) 897-0500
Facsimile: (212) 697-2521
www.novicklawgroup.com

Richard Alan Chen, Esq.
41-60 Main Street, Suite 203
Flushing, New York 11355

Re: Estate of Sydney Fields File No. 2016-111

Dear Mr. Chen:

We received the enclosed documents from your client, who claims that he is pro se. Since we have

App.91a

not received a consent to change attorneys for matters before the Surrogate's Court, we are addressing this matter to you.

The enclosed documents are hereby rejected and are being returned to Objectants' counsel for non-compliance with the CPLR.

Very truly yours,

/s/ Albert V. Messina, Jr.

Enclosure

cc: Jules M. Haas, Esq.
    Edward R. Curtin, Esq.
    Lisa Barbieri, Esq.
    New York County Surrogate's Court:
    Probate Department
    Diana Palmeri

App.92a

APPENDIX D
DEPOSITION FOR PIA FIELDS & DATA SHE PROVIDED

App.93a

DEPOSITION FOR PIA FIELDS AND HER DATA

[Pia Fields Deposition–Transcript, p.51]

... me. I think I want to give them a hand.

MR. HAAS: We could mark this as—not Petitioner's 3—fine, we'll mark this as Petitioner's 3.

(Petitioner's Exhibit 3, four-page typed notes, marked for identification, as of this date.)

MR. CHEN: I haven't read it. I heard what the witness said. I'll reserve objections, but otherwise fine.

MR. HAAS: So I'm going to take a two-minute break to make copies of this paper. I'll be right back.

If anybody needs to take a break for a minute and then I'll be right back.

(Brief recess taken.)

BY MR. HAAS:

Q. So Miss Fields, we were beginning to speak about this paper that you brought to today's deposition that you were referring to; am I correct?

A. Yes.

[. . .]

So just on this background I believe all his—and he once told Richard and me that all his life he worked to bring up his family to a middle class.

So impossible that he put all his family members away—behind and give all his money to somebody who have no related with him. That's my main point.

App.94a

Q. And that point that you—that you make is just based on your belief, correct?

A. Belief—based on the person's family background and his goal, his life goal.

Q. Whose life's goal?

A. Sydney Fields' life's goal.

Because he was living in a family without a father, he tried to be a good father, to bring his family life up. Okay? That's commonsense.

Q. But that's not based on anything that Sydney Fields ever told you; is that correct?

A. Yes. I never talked to Richard Fields—I never talked to Sydney Fields after Richard Fields walk away from our family. That's unfortunate. Because Sydney Fields said if he see us he have to see us—three of us together.

Because Richard is crazy, we lost the chance to contact Sydney Fields.

Q. So anything that you state with respect to what you think about Sydney Fields is based on your own personal feeling; is that correct?

A. Correct.

Q. But it's not based on anything that Sydney Fields ever told you; is that correct?

A. Sydney—yeah, Sydney Fields told us he work all his life to bring up the family to the middle class. That's my—my judgment is based on what he told me many years ago.

Q. And when did he tell that to you?

App.95a

A. Before—before he tried to stop Richard walk away.

He told us he work hard for the family. Richard should not ruin what he works for the family and just walk away.

Q. But that was in 1991 or before 1991; am I correct?

A. Yeah.

Q. This paper that we're talking about here, Petitioner's 3, did you show this paper to Richard? Ever show this paper to Richard Fields?

A. No. I think—I didn't talk to him, because I don't want him to remind all those sad stories.

Q. I'm sorry, I didn't understand that.

A. I don't want him to remind how he lost his home, how he come back to us for help, how he cut my hands. I don't want him to remind that, so I just write it myself.

Q. Down here, if you take a look at the end here, in paragraph 14, in that last paragraph, it says, I do not mind how much I will spend. I promise his mother to take care of Richard.

What does that mean?

A. I mean because Richard has money—have no money to pay the legal fee, I'm the one who pay for him.

I cannot see people step on him, take all his money and not give him a hand. I will regret if I not give him a hand. Okay? The rest of life I will regret.

App.96a

Q. So based on what you testified to, you had no contact with Sydney Fields in the year 2014, correct?

A. 2014—no. After Richard Fields walk away, I never have a chance to contact him—talk to him and see him.

Q. That was 1991?

A. 1991, correct.

It's because Richard is crazy. Messed up all the family relationship.

Q. Okay.

MR. HAAS: Let me mark something else here.

[. . .]

App.97a

PIA FIELDS PROVIDES IN DEPOSITION (EXHIBIT THREE)

1. Introduce your self
2. Where do you know Richard Fields?

   In Hunter College, summer class.

   – How soon do you get marry?

   Eight days.

   – Is any reason you make decision so fast?

   He told me what happen in his family that touch me deeply.

   His father was born one day after his grandfather died. That was a fluid in 1918 killed over one million people. A same doctor signed the death certificate and birth certificate. He risk his life to save a new born baby. That picture touch me. I also thought of feel of the Sydney's mother, watch her husband's dead body was carried out when giving her baby born. I decide to give this family a hand, helping the lady's grandson. I once regret for my decision and consider that is overreact, wasting my twenty years for an old story. Today when I sitting to defend the family's asset I realize that everything is predestined. This family deed need my help one hundred after.

3. Did you see Sydney before you marry Richard?

   No, Richard took me to Central Park west, he refuse to see us. Richard cried lowed in the park, he said his mother was crazy and his father ignore him. That moment I decide to take care of him.

App.98a

4. Do you know why Sydney refuse to see Richard?

Actually Sydney was a good father because he know the sadness a family without a father. He worked very hard, 70 hours a week. He once told Richard that I work for you and you not appreciate it. Gladys once walk away from her job and had not income to pay rent. Sydney waited for Richard at the outside of the building telling him that he will be a homeless soon. Richard ignore him and walk he drive his car to follow and convince him.

Later after that he arrange Richard in a small apartment in Manhattan, let him work in Bolton and study in Hunter. He seeing Richard a few times a week. One day the gas pipe in the room leaking gas. Richard's mother told Richard that his father tried to kill him. Richard believe that ran away from Sydney and wrote letter to accuse him. They did not see each for a few years.

5. When did Sydney see Richard again?

1989 one year before Lewis was born. We flied to Californian to Visit Uncle Solomon. After that Sydney seeing us. He was happy to see Richard's GED is 4. He asked us for a few times who's idea to put our marriage news in NY time because he did know that through his clients.

6. How about his relationship with Lewis?

He told Richard that he could not sleep the night Lewis was born. He came to the hospital to see Lewis. He was strangle by a chair when rush to the window of the infant's room. Lewis was named after Sydney's grandfather. Sydney growth up in his grandfather's home and he knew how close the relationship between grandfather and grandchildren could be. He never live in the same city with Kenny's children and did not watch them growth up. Yet for seeing them he even try to filed a court case. It poofs his love to his grandchildren more than the regular grandfathers. He once told Richard that if Richard had child with any woman should let him know even though he never get marry the mother.

7. How often he seeing you then?

Once a week he see Lewis. Every time talk with us on phone, he said how are you, without hearing our answer he asked how was Lewis. When he saw us, he walk strait to Lewis and cannot wait to carry him.

8. What happen make you stop to see each other?

He arranged an appointment without telling us what was that about? When got into a building with security guard Richard felt very angry, he used his pen to scratch the form he fill out. Later we realized that was a mental hospital. That hospital wanted to keep Richard as an inpatient that day. As his wife I have right to object it. I took Richard home and Richard run away from us soon after that.

Before that I heard their conversation through a speak phone. Sydney telling Richard I work all my life for bring the family to a middle class. You walk away from you wife and got disease you will rude in everything. I was surprised that family was so important in his mind. He said he will only see three of us together. Unfortunately, since Richard believe his father wanted to shut him in mental hospital he ran away from us we could never see Sydney again. That is a half month before Lewis was one year old. Still Sydney sent Lewis a check at Lewis' birth day. I not

App.100a

tent to keep documents. Up to today I could not even locate the pictures that showing how proud Sydney was when he holding Lewis. It is predestine that after moving a few times the check copy was sitting right in my draw. That signature in the check was different from the Will and it encourage me to start this case.

9. Did you tried to contact Sydney after that?

I did. I sent pictures, cards, tapes record to him once a while until Lewis was eight years old. We never receive answers. That frustrated us. We stop for a few years and try contact when Lewis was enrolled to Bronx Science. When I read his first will I notice that even though he did not answer us all those years, he left 15% of his asset to Lewis in 1996 and put me as Lewis' guardian.

10. Did he ever respond you?

Only once. I told Sydney that in a few week Richard ate a bag of 50 cent as a meal because he had no money. When Gladys was about 86 years old, she could not take care of Richard anymore. She walked into a police department and asked for helping. She was arranged in a senior home and they not let Richard visit her. She cannot take care of Richard financially any more. Richard did not tell me the situation and just ask for twenty dollars every two weeks. I gave him. I did not known that he used that to buy food, one meal for one bag of potato chips cost 50 cents. I told Sydney the situation and hoped him to pay Gladys in time on that way Gladys had money to take care of Richard. He sent me a receive showing that everything was paid.

Actually money Sydney pay to Gladys gave no help to Richard. Gladys did save $20,000 at the time

App.101a

she was died. The money all go to the government because Richard could not claim that in time. The nursing home stop Richard visit Gladys for they believe Richard was craze and took advantage from his mother. We did not visited his mother anymore since then. When I move the senior center lost our contact. I rethink the whole situation, even though they told us she was dying we could not see her because Richard was in mental hospital then and I prefer she still believe that everything was OK for Richard.

11. After Richard ran away in 1991 when did he contact you again?

1994, the day before Sydney took Richard to the court, Richard asked me to back him up and didn't tell me what happened. We stay in the court for a short time and case was closed. Richard believed his father also hired a lawyer for him. He was considered violence and only needed to work certain hours for the community. I thought his father just gave him a lesson, prevent him commit crime and rude in his life. That can explain why in his 1996 will, two years after he received Richard's pictures he still gave Richard something. Even though the amount is only 35,000$ that was much more than 5,000$, amount that he gave to most of Palmeri's family members. In that Will beside the charity he gave all his money to his family like most of the Jewish people did. He was 80 years old then had clear mind and good health. Strong enough to insist his Will.

App.102a

12. Did Richard ask for help beside that after he walked away from you?

1991, after Richard went back to his mother and they moved right away. I had no way to locate him. Beside asked me go to the court with him. He knock my door at a snow night and that was the biggest snow since 1920. He lost his shelter for a few days already. I did not believe and walked 12 blocks in the snow to his apartment. We saw a note stick on his door by martial. He got rob and lost all his ID, shit in his pent and old bread in his bag. Next day we spent 4 hours to visit his mother who was in a nursing home of New Jessy. She was sent to Elmhurst mental hospital when hang out on the street and was settled in there. She believed it was Sydney kidnap her.

She told me that her heart was cut to piece when she saw Richard visit her, took a shower and then went back to street. The center called policemen and still could not keep Gladys there. I took her back to New York and settled them in a family motel room. I lend them money that weekend. When the bank opened she returned me the money she throw me out of that room. She was an angry and crazy woman, yield and curse every minute. All her topics were about Sydney. They lived in there another 2 years and did not contact me, until Gladys was caught to hospital again. The motel owner called me and told me that Richard lost help from his mother, he could not even take care of his daily life.

We located his mother again in a senior center of Qgarden. I arranged them in a studio of my building till Gladys decided to move to senior center in 2007. I had no choice and took Richard back home after he was released from Elmhurst hospital mental depart-

App.103a

ment. He behaviors ok in the beginning but getting worse and worse again. He used hand to make gun pointing to the children in my building and slammed doors in front of people. Lewis did not like Richard for he felt humiliated to be his son. He hit Richard one day for he believed that Richard ate his Yogurt. His Yogurt was found in the refrigerator later. Richard ran away desperately from Lewis since that. I rented a place for Lewis in Manhattan. It was too late. One day Richard mummer and got into my room with a knife. He pointed my throats with the knife. I used my hand to stop him and my thumb got 12 ditches in the hospital later.

Richard was caught by the policemen. I did not prosecute him and the court order him got treatment since then. That was 2009.

13. How do you think about the relationship between Richard and Sydney?

Richard felt proud of his father. He believed his father should send him to law school and Sydney told him to see psychiatrist instead. That is the reason they can never get compromise. Sydney had no addicts about drug, gamble or alcohol. He was not like those people never know they had children, never care about their children and never think of inherit to their children. Sydney once file court case to see his grandchildren. If Sydney believed Richard did not need money and gave all his asset to charity or to the woman he loved, we have nothing to say. Now Palmeri' family telling us that Sydney not give money to Richard because Richard threaten his father. The fact is that Richard is mental disorder. This should be another story for our law protect people who are insane.

App.104a

Beside that Sydney owe Richard a health growing environment. He tricked Gladys sign a no fault divorce paper in Mexico and save a lot of money. Gladys did not accept it and spent all her saving in 25 years to defend her marriage. Richard watching her crying since he was a helpless 3 years old kid. She put food on the table for Richard like feeding a cat. She herself walked 100 blocks in the winter. Sydney sent Kenny mother to mental hospital and never let her see her child again. She complained that he sold her house that her father gave her. Kenny not seeing Sydney might be because find out these truths.

I don't mean to say who is right who is wrong at this moment. It is obvious that if his first two wives were not craze, if he handled the divorces little bit fairly, the relationships between him and his children would be not so mass up. Nobody could take advantage from them like they are doing now. I believe American law will consider the whole situation and not just see if there were witness seeing Sydney sign some paper.

14. What else make you support Richard to challenge the Will?

As what I said above I believe our law will protect a family that have three people insane. Beside that I don't believe Sydney would accuse Lewis refuse to see him. We tried to contact him from 1991 to till 2005. When my father died Lewis a very nice letter, saying that he realized how valuable family relationship was. He got no answer, maybe because Sydney was blind already and could not read the small words anymore. Maybe someone kept the letter from him. However, I still remember when we had coffee after we walk out of the mental hospital. He

App.105a

gazing Lewis and looked so sad. He known clearly that Lewis could not see him is because Richard insane and walked away. No matter in what situation he would not accuse Lewis except he lost his mind or someone made up the will. That is another reason I support Richard challenge the Will.

I do not mind how much I will spend. I promise his mother to take care of Richard. Lost inherit from his father Richard's life would be short for ten years. In the coming decades when I buy food and clothes for Richard it will remind me that I am a looser for I did not giving him a hand when I saw people rob him. There for I decide pay and see how people step on a disability person, took away his father's 10 million dollars walk away from this court room and let the government pay for everything Richard needs.

App.106a

APPENDIX E
DOCUMENTS WITH FORGERY AND MISTAKES

App.107a

CURT BAGGET HANDWRITING ANALYSIS (OCTOBER 13, 2017)

HANDWRITING EXPERT, LLC
Curt Baggett
Expert Document Examiner
908 Audelia Road, Suite 200-245
Richardson, Texas 75081
Phone: (972) 644-0285
Fax: (972) 644-5233
cbhandwritng@gmail.com
www.ExpertDocumentExaminer.com

Questioned Document Examiner Letter

Subject: Sydney H. Fields

I have examined three (3) documents with the known signatures of Sydney Fields. For the purpose of this examination I have labeled these exhibits 'K1' through 'K3'.

Today I have compared the signatures of Sydney H. Fields on the 'K' documents to the SHF initials on the questioned document, identified herein as 'Q2', to determine if the author of the Sydney H. Fields signatures on the 'K' documents was the same person who authored the initials of SHF on the questioned document: Typed Last Will and Testament, Initials bottom of Page 1.

An examination of handwriting includes establishing patterns of writing habits to help identify the author. Handwriting is formed by repeated habits of writing by the author, which are created by neuropathways established in the brain. These neuropathways control muscular and nerve movement for writing, whether the writing done is by the hand, foot or mouth.

In support of my opinion, I have included an excerpt from *Handwriting Identification, Facts and Fundamentals* by Roy A. Huber and A.M. Headrick (CRC Press LLC, 1999, pp 50-51) wherein the leading forefathers of document exan1ination in the USA agree that one significant difference in the fundamental structure of a writing compared to another is enough to preclude common authorship:

> [Ordway] Hilton stated: "It is basic axiom of identification in document problems that a limited number of basic differences, even in the face of numerous strong similarities, are controlling and accurately establish non-identity."

> [Wilson R.] Harrison made similar comments: " . . . the fundamental rule which admits of no exception when handwritings are being compared . . . is simple—whatever features two specimens of handwriting may have in common, they cannot be considered to be of common authorship if they display but a single consistent dissimilarity in any feature which is fundamental to the structure of the handwriting, and whose presence is not capable of reasonable explanation."

> [James V.P.] Conway expressed the same theme when he wrote: "A series of fundamental agreements in identifying individualities is requisite to the conclusion that two writings were authored by the same

App.109a

person, whereas a single fundamental difference in an identifying individuality between two writings precludes the conclusion that they were executed by the same person."

and finally,

[Albert S.] Osborn and others have generally agreed that despite numerous similarities in two sets of writings, a conclusion of identify cannot be made if there is one or more differences in fundamental features of the writings.

Based upon thorough analysis of these items, and from an application of accepted forensic document examination tools, principles and techniques, it is my professional expert opinion that a different person authored the initials of SHF on the questioned document. Someone did indeed forge the initials of SHF on the questioned document, 'Q2'. (App.113a)

I am willing to testify to this fact in a court of law and I will provide exhibits to the Court showing that I had sufficient data and that my opinion is correct. My Curriculum Vitae is attached and incorporated herein by reference.

Respectfully submitted,

/s/ Curt Baggett

App.110a

The above Letter Opinion was sworn and subscribed before me by Curt Baggett this 13th day of October, 2017.

State of Texas
County of Dallas

/s/ Patricia J. Hale
Notary Public, State of Texas
Comm. Expires 02-05-2020
Notary ID 130525886

App.111a

LAST WILL AND TESTAMENT OF SYDNEY H. FIELDS

I, SYDNEY H. FIELDS, residing at 372 Central Park West, Apartment 20P in the City, County and State of New York, being of sound and disposing mind and memory, do make, publish and declare this to be my Last Will and Testament, hereby revoking all prior wills and codicils made by me.

FIRST: I order and direct the payment of all my just debts and testamentary expenses as soon as practicable after my death.

SECOND: I direct that all inheritance, estate and any other tax in respect of any inheritance under this my last will and testament by reason of any State, Federal or other laws new or hereafter in force (including any interest and penalties thereon) shall be paid by my executor or alternate executor out of my residuary estate as part of the expenses of administration thereof without apportionment.

THIRD: I give and bequeath $500 to the CITY COLLEGE FUND of the CITY UNIVERSITY OF NEW YORK, $500 to the UNITED JEWISH APPEAL OF NEW YORK, and $1,000 to the BARUCH COLLEGE FUND of the CITY UNIVERSITY OF NEW YORK.

FOURTH: All the rest, residue and remainder of my property and estate, both real and personal of every kind and description and wheresoever situated which shall belong to me or be subject to my disposal at the time of my death (my residuary estate) I give and bequeath as follows:

    A.   20% (twenty percent) to OLGA PALMERI, currently residing at 80 Forest Avenue,

Paramus, NJ 07652. If she should predecease me, I leave her share of my residuary estate to VICTOR PALMERI, Sr.

B. 35% (thirty-five percent) to DIANA PALMERI, currently residing at 750 Ridgewood Avenue, Oradel, NJ 07649. If she should predecease me, I leave her share in equal percentages to her husband, DAVID and each of their three children, with DAVID to act as Trustee of the shares left to their children until they reach majority.

C. 20% (twenty percent) to VICTOR PALMERI, Jr., currently residing at 80 Forest Avenue, Paramus NJ 07652. If he should predecease me, I leave his share to OLGA PALMERI.

D. 15% (fifteen percent) to CYNTHIA PALMERI, currently residing at 80 Forest Avenue, Paramus NJ 07652. If she should predecease me, I leave her share in equal shares to each of her children, per stirpes.

E. 10% (ten percent) to ANA MARIA GARZON YEPEZ, currently residing at Francisco Oliva Oe3-73 y Cap. Edmundo Chiriboga Casa #46, Quito, Ecuador, or her heirs if she should predecease me.

App.113a

FOURTH: All the rest, residue and remainder of my property and estate, both real and personal of every kind and description and wheresoever situated which shall belong to me or be subject to my disposal at the time of my death (my residuary estate) I give and bequeath as follows:

  A. 20% (twenty percent) to OLGA PALMERI, currently residing at 80 Forest Avenue, Paramus, NJ 07652. If she should predecease me, I leave her share of my residuary estate to VICTOR PALMERI, Sr.
  B. 35% (thirty-five percent) to DIANA PALMERI, currently residing at 750 Ridgewood Avenue, Oradel, NJ 07649. If she should predecease me, I leave her share in equal percentages to her husband, DAVID and each of their three children, with DAVID to act as Trustee of the shares left to their children until they reach majority.
  C. 20% (twenty percent) to VICTOR PALMERI, Jr., currently residing at 80 Forest Avenue, Paramus NJ 07652. If he should predecease me, I leave his share to OLGA PALMERI.
  D. 15% (fifteen percent) to CYNTHIA PALMERI, currently residing at 80 Forest Avenue, Paramus NJ 07652. If she should predecease me, I leave her share in equal shares to each of her children, per stirpes.
  E. 10% (ten percent) to ANA MARIA GARZON YEPEZ, currently residing at Francisco Oliva Oe3-73 y Cap. Edmundo Chiriboga Casa #46, Quito, Ecuador, or her heirs if she should predecease me.

App.114a

CHECK IMAGES

IMAGE 1

App.115a

Image 2

App.116a

IMAGE 3

App.117a

CURT BAGGET CURRICULUM VITAE

CURT BAGGETT
EXPERT DOCUMENT EXAMINER
908 Audelia Road, Suite 200-245
Richardson, Texas 75081
Phone: (972) 644-0285 – Fax: (972) 644-5233
cbhandwritng@gmail.com
www.ExpertDocumentExaminer.com

Curt Baggett is a leading handwriting expert in the United States. He is also a skilled authority in document examination and as an expert witness and he has completed over 5,000 cases. Mr. Baggett has examined documents and/or testified in court cases as a handwriting expert in all 50 states, Washington, D.C., the Bahamas, Brazil, Canada, Chile, England, Ireland, Mexico, Pakistan, Puerto Rico, Thailand and New Zealand, Korea, China, Australia and Denmark.

The U.S. Department of Justice, the State of Arizona, State of Arkansas, the State of California, Louisiana Public Defender Board, and the State of Texas have retained him. Mr. Baggett has appeared as a handwriting expert on WOLF-BLITZER-CNN; CHARLES GIBSON-ABC, INSIDE EDITION, CBS Network Radio, CBS, CNBC, CNN, FOX, JUDGE ALEX, TEXAS JUSTICE and GOOD MORNING TEXAS and was a consultant as a forensic document examiner for a number one television show, "CSI: Crime Scene Investigation". Mr. Baggett is the co-author of "The Handwriting Certification Home Study Course" and "How to Spot a Forgery" and has been a guest on various other television and radio programs discussing handwriting and forensic document examination.

App.118a

Mr. Baggett once held the position as Dean of the School of Forensic Document Examination at Handwriting University. In addition to lecturing and teaching document examination, Mr. Baggett has analyzed handwriting for over 40 years. He has been qualified as an expert witness in Justice of the Peace, Municipal, District, State, U.S. District, and Federal Bankruptcy Courts, Eastern Caribbean Supreme Court, High Court of Tynwald British Isles and the Provincial Courts of Canada.

His education and training in document examination and psychology include: U.S. Army, Military Police Officer's School; B.A. and M.Ed., McNeese State University, Lake Charles, Louisiana; and post-graduate studies at the University of Houston, Houston, Texas.

Curt Baggett's library is extensive and includes literature on questioned document examination, forensic handwriting analysis, behavior profiling, and statement analysis.

Laboratory equipment used for examination consists of a Stereo Star Zoom American Optical 7x-30x twin microscope; Micronta illuminated 30x microscope; stereo microscope S/ST series; universal DigiScoping adapter; numerous magnifying devices; protractor and metric measuring devices; Pentax ME camera; Pentax macro 1.4, 50mm flat copy lens; overhead projector; light table, and transparencies.

Curt Baggett's Education and Training in Handwriting and Document Examination Include:

An in person two-year apprenticeship with Dr. Ray Walker as a handwriting expert and questioned document examiner. Dr. Walker's qualifications have been affirmed in the Court of Appeals, Fifth District of Texas at Dallas, and had historical rulings in his favor. A leading authority in the field of handwriting analysis and document examination, Dr. Walker is the author of The Questioned Document Examiner and the Justice System.

The American Bureau of Document Examiners certifies Mr. Baggett. He also has a certificate of completion from the American Institute of Applied Science.

[. . .]

CHECK IMAGES

IMAGE 1

Vanguard® GNMA Fund
Admiral Shares

SYDNEY H FIELDS
372 CENTRAL PARK W, APT. 20P
NEW YORK NY 10025-8213

1001

DATE 9/10/14

PAY TO THE ORDER OF Walter B. Cooke $ 10,297.25

Ten Thousand and Two Hundred Ninety Nine 25/100 DOLLARS

NOT VALID FOR LESS THAN $250.00

Payable Through
Wachovia Bank, National Association
Wilmington, DE 19803

FOR

X Sydney H Fields X

⑈105360100 19⑈⑆031100225⑆850097137648 18⑈

IMAGE 2

Vanguard® New York
Tax-Exempt
Money Market Fund

SYDNEY H. FIELDS
372 CENTRAL PARK W, APT. 20P
NEW YORK NY 10025-8213

1228

PER ENV

DATE 12/10/14

PAY TO THE ORDER OF Mt. Sinai Hospital $ 264.00/100

Two Hundred Sixty Four Dollars 00/100 DOLLARS

NOT VALID FOR LESS THAN $250.00

Payable Through
Wachovia Bank, National Association Teresa Fields
Wilmington, DE 19803

FOR Acct # [redacted] 602

X Sydney H Fields

⑈101630 1228⑈⑆031100225⑆850097137648 18⑈ ⑈0000026400⑈

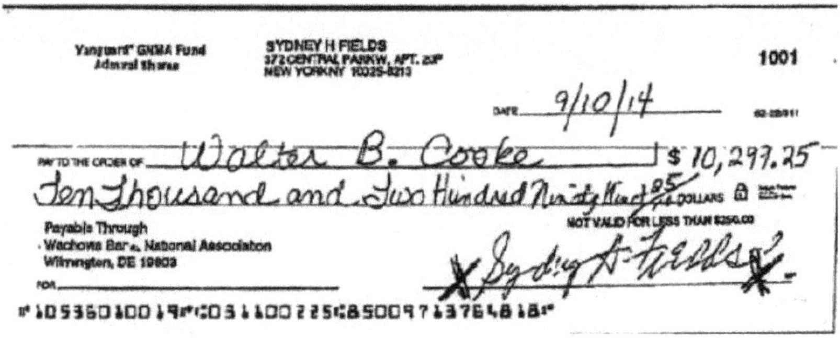

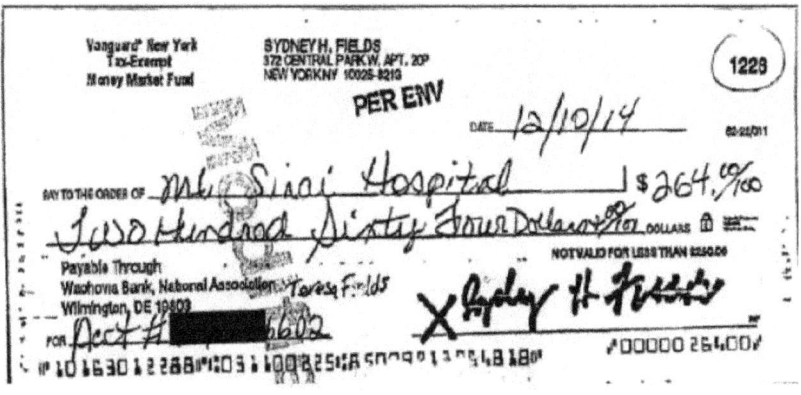

App.121a

TESTATOR'S HANDWRITTEN NOTE FOR THE PROBATE BILL (OCTOBER 8, 2013)

Olga Palmeri	20
Diana Palmeri	40
Ana M. Garzon	10
Victor Palmeri	15
Cynthia Palmeri	<u>15</u>
	100

App.122a

1965

OLGA PALMIERI — 20
DIANA PALMIERI 40
ANITA 'N GARZON 10
VICTOR PALMIERI 15
CYNTHIA PALMIERI 15
───
100

App.123a

IN WITNESS WHEREOF, I have subscribed and sealed and do publish and declare these presents as and for my Last Will and Testament, in the presence of the witnesses attesting the same at my request, this 6th day of October, 2014.

x _Sydney H. Fields_ (L.S.)
SYDNEY H. FIELDS

ON THIS 6th day of October, 2014, SYDNEY H. FIELDS, the above-named Testator, in our presence subscribed and sealed the foregoing instrument and declared the same to be her Last Will and Testament, and we, thereupon, at her request and in her presence and in the presence of each other, have hereunto subscribed our names as attesting witnesses.

Put her instead of His

Jill Curtin of _220 West 71st Street_
JILL CURTIN   _New York, NY 10023_

Susan Lehman of _220 W. 71st St. #32_
SUSAN LEHMAN   _New York, NY 10023_

CURTIN'S SCRATCH PAPER FOR PROBATED WILL

LAST WILL AND TESTAMENT OF SYDNEY H. FIELDS

I, SYDNEY H. FIELDS, residing at 372 Central Park West in the City, County and State of New York, Being of sound and disposing mind and memory, do make, publish and declare this to be my Last Will and Testament, hereby revoking all prior wills and codicils made up by me.

FIRST: I order and direct the payment of all my just debts and testamentary expenses as soon as practicable after my death.

SECOND: I direct that all inheritance, estate and any other tax in respect of any inheritance under this my last will and testament by reason of any State, Federal or other laws now or hereafter in force (including any interest and penalties thereon) shall be paid by my executrix or alternate executor out of my residuary estate as part of the expenses of administration thereof without apportionment. JH SON / TRUST

TO CHILDREN PER STIRPES — DAVID 3 KIDS

THIRD: All the rest, residue and remainder of my property and estate, both real and personal of every kind and description and wheresoever situated which shall belong to me or be subject to my disposal at the time of my death (my residuary estate) I give devise and bequeath as follows:

— ROBERT, 20%
ROSE PLUMB, 35% — CERT 80 EAST AVE, PARAMUS
NIECE BARBARA W. GATTON, 10% — IF PREDCSD SEE FILES 756 RIDGEWOOD AVE, ORADEL, N.J. 07649
VICTOR PLUMB, JR., 20% — TO FOREST AVE, PARAMUS NJ 07652
CYNTHIA PLUMB, 15% — 80 FOXES " "
→ TO CHILDREN IF PREDECSD
→ GOES TO YEN IF PREDECSD

App.125a

Handwritten at top left: H1: Curtin's Scratch Paper For Probated Will

LAST WILL AND TESTAMENT OF SYDNEY H. FIELDS

1941

I, SYDNEY H. FIELDS, residing at 372 Central Park West in the City, County and State of New York, Being of sound and disposing mind and memory, do make, publish and declare this to be my Last Will and Testament, hereby revoking all prior wills and codicils made up by me.

FIRST: I order and direct the payment of all my just debts and testamentary expenses as soon as practicable after my death.

SECOND: I direct that all inheritance, estate and any other tax in respect of any inheritance under this my last will and testament by reason of any State, Federal or other laws new or hereafter in force (including any interest and penalties thereon) shall be paid by my executrix or alternate executor out of my residuary estate as part of the expenses of administration thereof without apportionment.

THIRD: I give, devise and bequeath all of my right, title and interest in and to the condominium unit presently owned and occupied by me known as apartment 20P in the building located at 372 Central Park West, New York, New York (located in Manhattan – Block 1833 – Lot 2406) together with the contents thereof to my beloved wife, TERESA FIELDS. In addition to the foregoing, I give and bequeath to my said wife TERESA FIELDS a sum equal to one-half (1/2) of my remaining gross estate computed with deductions for the condominium apt. #20P at 372 Central Park West, New York, NY 10025, if she shall survive me. In the event my wife TERESA FIELDS does not survive me, my entire right, title and interest in and to said condominium and its contents shall be disposed of as part of my residuary estate as provided herein.

FOURTH: I give and bequeath to the following named persons, if living at the time of my death

A. To my nephew VICTOR PALMERI, Jr., my Rolex watch (model #18038), my only pinky ring, and the sum of Thirty-Five Thousand Dollars ($35,000); *HAWAII 15%*

B. To the children of my niece CYNTHIA PALMERI, the sum of Five Thousand Dollars ($5,000) each; *15%*

C. To the children of my niece DIANA PALMERI LUKAC, the sum of Five Thousand Dollars *40% NE*

D. ~~To LEWIS O. FIELDS, my grandson, the sum of Thirty-Five Thousand Dollars ($35,000)~~ *(circled 2)*

Handwritten:
OLGA PALMERI 20%   PARAMOS N.J.
DIANA PALMERI 30%
ANITA A. GARZON 10%   ECUADOR S.A.

FIFTH: (a) Because my son Kenneth L. Fields refused to let me visit my grandchildren, Elizabeth and Alex P. Fields and refused to have a relationship with me even after a lawsuit where I sought visitation rights, I deliberately make no provision for him in this Will and it is my intention that he receive no part of my estate.

(b) Because my son Richard Fields hired a lawyer to sue me for money and because I had to have him arrested and brought to court for harassment of me and my wife, Teresa I deliberately make no provision for him in this Will and it is my intention that he receive no part of my estate.

(c) Because my grandchildren Elizabeth and Alex P. Fields refused to have a relationship with me after reaching adulthood, I deliberately make no provision for either one in this will and it my intention that neither receive any part of my estate.

SIXTH: All the rest, residue and remainder of my property and estate, both real and personal, of every kind and description and wheresoever situated, which shall belong to me or be subject to my disposal at the time of my death (my residuary estate) I give devise and bequeath as follows:

To the trustee hereinafter named, in trust, for the following uses and purposes: To hold, manage invest and reinvest the same, to collect the income therefrom to or for the benefit of my wife TERESA FIELDS and to distribute the income therefrom to my wife at such times and in such amounts as the Trustees shall in their absolute discretion determine. It is my intention that the principal of the trust established pursuant to Article Sixth shall not be invaded for the benefit of my wife TERESA FIELDS except to the extent that she has extraordinary hardship as determined by the Trustees in their absolute discretion.

Upon the death of TERESA FIELDS the undistributed principal and interest of the trust established pursuant to this Article Sixth, net of all estate, income and other taxes and all trustees' fees and commissions payable shall be distributed by the Trustees as follows:

$500 →
$500
$1000

A. Twenty Five percent (25%) to the CITY COLLEGE FUND of the CITY UNIVERSITY of NEW YORK.
B. Ten percent (10%) to the UNITED JEWISH APPEAL of NEW YORK.
C. Fifty percent (50%) to my nephew VICTOR PALMERI, JR. shall he survive me.
D. Fifteen percent (15%) to the BARUCH COLLEGE FUND of the CITY UNIVERSITY of NEW YORK.

I hereby designate and appoint my wife TERESA FIELDS and my nephew VICTOR PALMERI, JR. as Co-Trustees of the Trust to be established pursuant to this Article Sixth.

be disposed of ~~by my by my alternate executor as specified in sections (A) through (D) of this article sixth without necessity of establishing a trust~~

SEVENTH: In the event that my wife TERESA FIELDS ~~and myself~~ die in a common accident, it shall be ~~assumed~~ that I survived her and bequests ~~made to her in this will~~ shall be deemed to be part of my residuary estate, except for the contents of our residence at 372 Central Park West ~~which~~ shall be deemed to be part of her estate under such circumstances.

DIANA PALMERI

EIGHTH: I hereby nominate constitute and appoint my beloved wife, ~~TERESA FIELDS~~, executrix of this my Last Will and Testament, and I direct that no bond or other security shall be required of her (or any alternate executor or any co-trustee hereunder) for the faithful performance of her fiduciary duties hereunder in any jurisdiction.

OLGA

VICTOR PALMERI SR.

In the event that my wife ~~TERESA FIELDS~~ shall predecease me, or if she is unwilling or unable to serve as my executrix for any reason whatsoever then I nominate constitute and appoint my nephew VICTOR PALMERI, JR. as alternate executor with like powers and immunities.

~~In the event that my nephew, VICTOR PALMERI, JR. also predeceases me, or if he is unwilling or unable to serve as alternate executor for any reason whatsoever I nominate constitute and appoint US TRUST COMPANY an alternate executor.~~

In addition to the powers and authority conferred on executors by law, and to enable my executrix or alternate executor to liquidate and distribute my estate in a prompt and orderly manner, I authorize and empower my executrix and alternate executor to do everything she or he deems necessary or desirable for the proper execution or discharge of any powers or duties held by or imposed on her or him by this will or by applicable law, even though it would not be authorized or appropriate for fiduciaries under any statute or rule of law, including the power to maintain, sell, pledge mortgage, lease transfer, exchange, convert or otherwise dispose of any property in my estate, to make sales publicly or privately wholly or partly on credit, delegate discretionary powers to agents, remunerate them and pay their expenses, distribute in kind or in money or partly to each compromise or otherwise adjust any claims or demands in favor of or against my estate, and to execute and deliver such instruments as may be necessary to carry out any of these powers, subject only to the duty to act in good faith and with responsible care.

NINTH: It is my wish to take full advantage of the unified credit and state death tax credit available to my estate (provided the use of such credit does not require an increase in the state death taxes payable) but no other credit, and after taking into account property disposed of by this will and property passing outside of this will which is includable in my gross estate and does not qualify for the marital or charitable deduction.

TENTH: ~~If any beneficiary other than my wife, TERESA FIELDS, shall~~ in any manner directly or indirectly, attempt to contest or oppose the validity of this will or commence, interested or instrumental in the institution or maintenance of any action or proceeding in any court for the purpose of preventing the probate of this will or for the purpose of attacking the validity of this will or any provision hereof, then in such event such beneficiary shall forfeit his or her share hereunder, all provisions in this will for the benefit of such contesting beneficiary shall be revoked, such contesting beneficiary and his or her descendants shall be deemed to have predeceased me and shall receive no part of my estate in intestacy or otherwise and all such benefits shall be disposed of as part of my residuary estate except to the extent such contesting beneficiary is a beneficiary of a share of my residuary estate, in which event such share shall be forfeited and apportioned pro rata among other beneficiaries sharing in my residuary estate.

ELEVENTH: ~~It is my wish that~~ upon my death, my body be ~~cremated and the ashes~~ be **Plot** given to my wife TERESA FIELDS for her disposal if she survives me. If ~~she~~ does not survive me, ~~the ashes should be given~~ to my nephew, VICTOR PALMIERI, JR. for his ~~disposal.~~ Buried at Family Plot, YCFC Cemetery, St. David, Queens NY

IN WITNESS WHEREOF, I have subscribed and sealed and do publish and declare these presents as and for my Last Will and Testament, in the presence of the witnesses attesting the same at my request, this   day of July in the year Two Thousand and Six.

_____ (L.S.)
SYDNEY H. FIELDS

ON THIS   day of July, 2006, SYDNEY H. FIELDS, the above-named Testator, in our presence subscribed and sealed the foregoing instrument and declared the same to be her Last Will and Testament; and we, thereupon, at her request and in her presence and in the presence of each other, have hereunto subscribed our names as attesting witnesses.

_____ of   _____
                                _____

_____ of   _____
                                _____

App.129a

Appendix: F

Sydney's Three Wills

App.130a

MAY 2, 1997 WILL

I SYDNEY H. FIELDS, residing at 372 Central Park West in the City, County and State of New York, being of sound and disposing mind and memory, do make, publish and declare this to be my Last Will and Testament, hereby revoking all prior Wills and Codicils made by me.

FIRST: I order and direct the payment of all my just debts, funeral and testamentary expenses as soon as practicable after my death. It is my wish that I be buried in the family plot at the YCFC Organization cemetery in Elmont, Long island.

SECOND: I direct that all inheritance, estate and any other tax in respect of any inheritance under this my Last Will and Testament by reason of any State, Federal or other laws now or hereafter in force (including any interest and penalties thereon), shall be paid by my Executrix or Alternate Executor out of my residuary estate as pan of the expenses of administration thereof without apportionment.

THIRD: I give, devise and bequeath all of my right, title and interest in and to the condominium unit presently owned and occupied by me, known as Apartment 20P in the building located at 372 Central Park West, New York, New York. Together with the contents thereof, and all of my right, title and interest in and to certain improved real property located at 706-712 North Avenue, New Rochelle, New York, to my wife, TERESA FIELDS, if she shall survive me. If she does not survive me, my entire right, title and interest in and to said condominium and its contents and said improved real property in New Rochelle shall be disposed of as a pan of my residuary estate as provided herein. In addition to the foregoing, I give and bequeath to my said wife TERESA FIELDS sum equal to one-third (1/3) of my gross estate.

FOURTH: I give and bequeath to the following named persons, if living at the time of my death:

- (A) To my nephew VICTOR PALMERI . . . the sum of Sixty-Five Thousand Dollars ($65,000) and my Rolex Watch (Model #18038).

- (B) To my niece CYNTHIA PALMERI, the sum of Five Thousand Dollars ($5,000).

- (C) To my niece DIANA PALMERI LUKAC, the sum of Five Thousand Dollars ($5,000).

- (D) To my uncle SOLOMON ROSEN, the sum of Thirty-Five Thousand Dollars ($35,000).

- (E) To my son RICHARD J. FIELDS, the sum of Thirty-Five Thousand Dollars ($35,000).

- (F) To the Trustee hereinafter named. in trust, for the benefit of my grandson LEWIS D. FIELDS, the sum of Thirty-Five Thousand Dollars ($35,000), to hold, invest and re-invest same and to collect the income therefrom until he shall attain the age of 21 years, at which time all principal and income in said trust shall be distributed to my said grandson. I hereby designate PIA FIELDS as such Trustee.

- (G) To the Trustee hereinafter named. in trust, for the benefit of my granddaughter ELIZABETH FIELDS, the sum of Thirty-Five Thousand Dollars ($35,000), to hold, invest and reinvest same and to collect the income therefrom until she shall attain the age of 25 years, at which time all principal and income in said must shall be distributed to my said granddaughter. I hereby designate VICTOR PALMERI, JR. as such Trustee.

(H) To the Trustee hereinafter named, in trust. for the benefit of my grandson ALEX P. FIELDS, the sum of Thirty-Five Thousand Dollars ($35,000), to hold, invest and reinvest same and to collect the income therefrom until he shall attain the age of 25, years, at which time all principal and income in said trust shall be distributed to my said grandson. I hereby designate VICTOR PALMERI, JR. as such Trustee.

If any beneficiary named in this Article FOURTH shall refuse his or her bequest, bequest hereunder such bequest shall be made as a charitable contribution to the CITY COLLEGE FUND of the City University of New York,

FIFTH: For reasons best know to my son KENNETH L. FIELDS, I deliberately make no provision for him in this Will, and it is my intention that he receive no pan of my estate.

SIXTH: All the rest, residue and remainder of my property and estate, both real and personal, of every kind and description and where so ever situated, which shall belong to me or be subject to my disposal at the time of my death (my "residuary estate"), I give, devise and bequeath as follows:

To the Trustees hereinafter named. in trust, for the following uses and purposes: to hold, manage,

App.133a

invest and reinvest the same, to collect the income therefrom to or for the benefit of my wife TERESA FIELDS and to distribute the income therefrom to my wife at such times and in such amounts as the Trustees shall in their absolute discretion determine. It is my intention that the principal of the Trust established pursuant to this Article SIXTH shall not be invaded for the benefit of my wife TERESA FIELDS except to the extent that she has extraordinary hardship as determined by the Trustees in their absolute discretion.

Upon the death of TERESA FIELDS, the undistributed principal and interest of the Trust established pursuant to this Article SIXTH, net of all estate, income and other taxes and all trustees' fees and commissions payable shall be distributed by the Trustees as follows:

(A) Twenty-Five Percent (25%) to the CITY COLLEGE FUND of the City University of New York.

(B) Ten Percent (10%) to the UNITED JEWISH

(C) Twenty-Five Percent (25%) to my granddaughter ELIZABETH FIELDS if she bas at such time attained the age of 35 years. or if not to the Trustee hereinafter named, in trust, for the benefit of my said granddaughter ELIZABETH FIELDS, to hold, invest and reinvest same and to collect the income therefrom until she shall attain the age of 35 years, at which time all principal and income in said trust shall be distributed to my said granddaughter. I hereby designate VICTOR PALMERI, JR. as such Trustee. In the event ELIZABETH FIELDS shall refuse

App.134a

her share of the Trust established pursuant to this Article SIXTH, but not before she reaches age 35, said funds shall be distributed to my son RICHARD J. FIELDS.

(D) Twenty-Five Percent (25%) to my grandson ALEX P. FIELDS if he has at such time attained the age of 35 years. of if not to the Trustee hereinafter named, in trust, for the benefit of my said grandson ALEX P. FIELDS, to hold, invest and reinvest same and to collect the income therefrom until he shall attain the age of 35 years, at which time all principal and income in said trust shall be distributed to my said grandson. I hereby designate VICTOR PALMERI, JR. as such Trustee. In the event ALEX P. FIELDS shall refuse his share of the Trust established pursuant to this Article SIXTH, but not before he reaches age 35, Sixty Percent (60%) of said share shall be distributed as a charitable contribution to the UNITED JEWISH APPEAL of New York, and Forty Percent (40%) of said share shall be distributed to my grandson LEWIS D. FIELDS if he has at such time attained the age of 21 years, or if not to the Trustee of the Trust established for the benefit of my grandson LEWIS D. FIELDS pursuant to Section (H) herein below.

(H) Fifteen Percent (15%) to my grandson LEWIS D. FIELDS if he has at such time attained the age of 21 years, of if not to the Trustee hereinafter named, in trust, for the benefit of my said grandson LEWIS D. FIELDS, to hold, invest and reinvest same and to collect the income therefrom until he shall attain the age of 21 years. at which time all principal and income in said trust shall be distributed 10 my said grandson. I hereby designate PIA FIELDS as such Trustee.

I hereby designate and appoint my wife TERESA FIELDS and my nephew VICTOR PALMERI, JR. as Trustees of the Trust to be established pursuant to this Article SIXTH.

In the event my wife TERESA FIELDS shall not survive me, my residuary estate shall be disposed of by my Alternate Executor as specified in Sections (A) through (H) of this Article SIXTH without the necessity of establishing a Trust.

SEVENTH: In the event that my wife TERESA FIELDS and myself die under such circumstances as to render it impossible to determine which of us survived. it shall be assumed that I survived her the bequests made to her in this Will shall be deemed to be part of my residuary estate except with respect to the contents of our residence at 372 Central Park West, which shall be deemed to be pan of her estate under such circumstances.

EIGHTH: I hereby nominate, constitute and appoint my beloved wife, TERESA FIELDS, Executrix of this my Last Will and Testament, and I direct that no bond or other security shall be required of her (or any Alternate Executor) for the faithful performance of her duties as Executrix in any jurisdiction.

In the event that my wife TERESA FIELDS shall predecease me, or if she is unwilling or unable to serve as my Executrix for any reason whatsoever, then I nominate, constitute and appoint my nephew VICTOR

App.136a

PALMERI, JR. as Alternate Executor with like powers and immunities.

In the event that my nephew VICTOR PALMERI, Jr. also predeceases me, or if he is unwilling or unable to serve as Alternate Executor for any reason whatsoever, I nominate, constitute and appoint U.S. TRUST COMPANY as Alternate Executor.

[. . .]

App.137a

JULY 27, 2006 WILL

I, SYDNEY H. FIELDS, residing at 372 Central Park West in the City, County and State of New York, Being of sound and disposing mind and memory, do make, publish and declare this to be my Last Will and Testament, hereby revoking all prior wills and codicils made up by me.

FIRST: I order and direct the payment of all my just debts and testamentary expenses as soon as practicable after my death.

SECOND: I direct that all inheritance, estate and any other tax in respect of any inheritance under this my last will and testament by reason of any State, Federal or other laws new or hereafter in force (including any interest and penalties thereon) shall be paid by my executrix or alternate executor out of my residuary estate as part of the expenses of administration thereof without apportionment.

THIRD: I give, devise and bequeath all of my right, title and interest in and to the condominium unit presently owned and occupied by me known as apartment 20P in the building located at 372 Central Park West, New York, New York (located in Manhattan-Block 1833-Lot 2406) together with the contents thereof to my beloved wife, TERESA FIELDS. In addition to the foregoing, I give and bequeath to my said wife TERESA FIELDS a sum equal to one-half (1/2) of my remaining gross estate computed with deductions for the condominium apt. #20P at 372 Central Park West, New York, NY 10025, if she shall survive me. In the event my wife TERESA FIELDS does not survive me, my entire right, title and interest in and to said condominium and its contents shall be disposed of as part of my residuary estate as provided herein.

FOURTH: I give and bequeath to the following named persons, if living at the time of my death

- A. To my nephew VICTOR PALMERI, JR., my Rolex watch (model #18038), my only pinky ring, and the sum of Thirty-Five Thousand Dollars ($35,000);
- B. To the children of my niece CYNTHIA PALMERI, the sum of Five Thousand Dollars ($5,000) each;
- C. To the children of my niece DIANA PALMERI LUKAC, the sum of Five Thousand Dollars ($5,000) each;
- D. To LEWIS D. FIELDS, my grandson, sum of Thirty-Five Thousand Dollars ($35,000); and
- E. To my uncle Solomon Rosen, the sum of Thirty-Five Thousand Dollars ($35,000).

FIFTH: (a) Because my son Kenneth L. Fields refused to let me visit my grandchildren, Elizabeth and Alex P. Fields and refused to have a relationship with me even after a lawsuit where I sought visitation rights, I deliberately make no provision for him in this Will and it is my intention that he receive no part of my estate.

(b) Because my son Richard Fields hired a lawyer to sue me for money and because I had to have him arrested and brought to court for harassment of me and my wife, Teresa I deliberately make no provision for him in this Will and it is my intention that he receive no part of my estate.

(c) Because my grandchildren Elizabeth and Alex P. Fields refused to have a relationship with me after reaching adulthood, I deliberately make no provision for either one in this will and it my intention that neither receive any part of my estate.

SIXTH: All the rest, residue and remainder of my property and estate, both real and personal of every kind and description and wheresoever situated which shall belong to me or be subject to my disposal at the time of my death (my residuary estate) I give devise and bequeath as follows:

To the trustee hereinafter named, in trust, for the following uses and purposes: To hold, manage invest and reinvest the same, to collect the income therefrom to or for the benefit of my wife TERESA FIELDS and to distribute the income therefrom to my wife at such times and in such amounts as the Trustees shall in their absolute discretion determine. It is my intention that the principal of the trust established pursuant to Article Sixth shall not be invaded for the benefit of my wife TERESA FIELDS except to the extent that she has extraordinary hardship as determined by the Trustees in their absolute discretion.

Upon the death of TERESA FIELDS the undistributed principal and interest of the trust established pursuant to this Article Sixth, net of all estate, income and other taxes and all trustees' fees and commissions payable shall be distributed by the Trustees as follows:

A. Twenty Five percent (25%) to the CITY COLLEGE FUND of the CITY UNIVERSITY of NEW YORK.

B. Ten percent (10%) to the UNITED JEWISH APPEAL of NEW YORK.

C. Fifty percent (50%) to my nephew VICTOR PALMERI, JR shall he survive me

D. Fifteen percent (15%) to the BARUCH COLLEGE FUND of the CITY UNIVERSITY OF NEW YORK.

I hereby designate and appoint my wife TERESA FIELDS and my nephew VICTOR PALMERI, JR as Co-Trustees of the Trust to be established pursuant to this Article Sixth.

... be disposed of my by my alternate executor as specified in sections (A) through (D) of this article sixth without necessity of establishing a trust.

SEVENTH: In the event that my wife TERESA FIELDS and myself die in a common accident, it shall be assumed that I survived her and bequests made to her in this will shall be deemed to be part of my residuary estate except for the contents of our residence at 372 Central Park West which shall be deemed to be part of her estate under such circumstances.

EIGHTH: I hereby nominate constitute and appoint my beloved wife, TERESA FIELDS, executrix of this my Last Will and Testament, and I direct that no bond or other security shall be required of her (or any alternate executor or any co-trustee hereunder) for the faithful performance of her fiduciary duties hereunder in any jurisdiction.

In the event that my wife TERESA FIELDS shall predecease me, or if she is unwilling or unable to serve as my executrix for any reason whatsoever then I nominate constitute and appoint my nephew VICTOR

App.141a

PALMERI, JR. as alternate executor with like powers and immunities.

In the event that my nephew, VICTOR PALMERI, JR. also predeceases my, or if he is unwilling or unable to serve as alternate executor for any reason whatsoever I nominate constitute and appoint US TRUST COMPANY as alternate executor.

In addition to the powers and authority conferred on executors by law, and to enable my executrix or alternate executor to liquidate and distribute my estate in a prompt and orderly manner, I authorize and empower my executrix and alternate executor to do everything she or he deems necessary or desirable for the proper execution or discharge of any powers or duties held by or imposed on her or him by this will or by applicable law, even though it would not be authorized or appropriate for fiduciaries under any statute or rule of law, including the power to maintain, sell, pledge mortgage, lease transfer, exchange, convert or otherwise dispose of any property in my estate, to make sales publicly or privately wholly or partly on credit, delegate discretionary powers to agents, remunerate them and pay their expenses, distribute in kind or in money or partly to each compromise or otherwise adjust any claims or demands in favor of or against my estate, and to execute and deliver such instruments as may be necessary to carry out any of these powers, subject only to the duty to act in good faith and with responsible care.

NINTH: It is my wish to take full advantage of the unified credit and state death tax credit available to my estate (provided the use of such credit does not require an increase in the state death taxes payable) but no other credit, and after taking into account property disposed of by this will and property passing outside of this will which is includable in my gross estate and does not qualify for the marital or charitable deduction.

TENTH: If any beneficiary other than my wife, TERESA FIELDS, shall in any manner directly or indirectly, attempt to contest or oppose the validity of this will or commence, interested or instrumental in the institution or maintenance of any action or proceeding in any court for the purpose of preventing the probate of this will or for the purpose of attacking the validity of this will or any provision hereof: then in such event such beneficiary shall forfeit his or her share hereunder, all provisions in this will for the benefit of such contesting beneficiary shall be revoked, such contesting beneficiary and his or her descendants shall be deemed to have predeceased me and shall receive no part of my estate in intestacy or otherwise and all such benefits shall be disposed of as part of my residuary estate except to the extent such contesting beneficiary is a beneficiary of a share of my residuary estate, in which event such share shall be forfeited and apportioned pro rata among other beneficiaries sharing in my residuary estate.

ELEVENTH: It is my wish that upon my death, my body be cremated and the ashes be given to my wife TERESA FIELDS for her disposal if she survives me. If she does not survive me, the ashes should be given to my nephew, VICTOR PALMERI, JR. for his disposal

IN WITNESS WHEREOF, I have subscribed and sealed and do publish and declare these presents as and for my Last Will and Testament, in the presence of the witnesses attesting the same at my request, this day of July in the year Two Thousand and Six.

App.143a

/s/ Sydney H. Fields

ON This 27th day of July, 2006, SYDNEY H. FIELDS, the above named Testator, in our presence subscribed and sealed the foregoing instrument and declared the same to be her Last Will and Testament; and we, thereupon, at her request and in her presence and in the presence of each other, have hereunto subscribed our names as attesting witnesses.

/s/ Jill Curtin
288 Lexington Ave.
New York, NY 10016

/s/ Daniel Curtin
288 Lexington Ave.
New York, NY 10016

App.144a

BACKUP DOCUMENT FOR THE WILL 2006 (HANDWRITTEN)

[. . .]

TENTH. If any Beneficiary other than my wife Teresa Fields shall in any manner directly or indirectly attempt to contest or oppose the validity of this will or commence, maintain or join in (except as a party Defendant), or be in any way directly or indirectly, interested or instrumental in the institution or maintenance of any action or proceeding in any court for the purpose of preventing the probate of this will or for the purpose of attacking the validity of this will or any provisions hereof, then in such event such beneficiary shall forfeit his or her share hereunder, all provisions in this will for the benefit of such contesting beneficiary shall be revoked such contesting beneficiary and his or her descendants shall be deemed to have predeceased me and shall receive no part of my estate in intestacy or otherwise, and all such benefits shall be disposed of as part of my residuary estate except to the extent such contesting beneficiary is a beneficiary of a share of my residuary estate, in which event such share shall be forfeited and apportioned pro rata among other beneficiaries sharing in my residuary estate.

ELEVENTH. It is my wish that upon my death my body be cremated and the ashes be given to my wife Teresa Fields for her disposal if she survives me. If she does not survive me, the ashes should be given to my nephew Victor Palmeri for his disposal.

Mr. Sydney H. Fields

App.145a

372 Central Park W Apt 20p
New York, NY 10025-8213
212-678-1494

IF ANY DAVID FICHART OTHER THAN HIS WIFE TERESA FIELDS SHALL IN ANY MANNER, DIRECTLY OR INDIRECTLY ATTEMPT TO CONTEST OR OPPOSE THE VALIDITY OF THIS WILL OR COMMENCE MAINTAIN OR JOIN IN ANY LEGAL ACT AS A PARTY DEFENDANT OR BE IN ANY WAY DIRECTLY OR INDIRECTLY INTERESTED OR INSTRUMENTAL IN THE INSTITUTION OR MAINTENANCE OF ANY ACTION OR PROCEEDING IN ANY COURT FOR THE PURPOSE OF PREVENTING THE PROBATE OF THIS WILL OR FOR THE PURPOSE OF ATTACKING THE VALIDITY OF THIS WILL OR ANY PROVISION HEREOF, THEN IN SUCH EVENT SUCH BENEFICIARY SHALL FORFEIT HIS OR HER SHARE HEREUNDER ALL PROVISIONS IN THIS WILL FOR THE BENEFIT OF SUCH CONTESTING BENEFICIARY SHALL BE REVOKED, AND CONTESTING BENEFICIARY AND HIS OR HER DESCENDANTS SHALL BE DEEMED TO HAVE PREDECEASED ME AND SHALL RECEIVE NO PART OF MY ESTATE IN INTESTACY OR OTHERWISE AND ALL SUCH BENEFITS

TFWJR

App.146a

SHALL BE disposed of as PART OF MY RESIDUARY ESTATE EXCEPT TO THE EXTENT SUCH CONTESTING BENEFICIARY IS A BENEFICIARY OF A SHARE OF MY RESIDUARY ESTATE IN WHICH EVENT SUCH SHARES SHALL BE FORFEITED AND A PROPORTIONATE PRO RATA AMONG OTHER BENEFICIARIES SHARING IN MY RESIDUARY ESTATE.

FOURTH IT IS MY WISH THAT UPON MY DEATH MY BODY BE CREMATED AND THE ASHES BE GIVEN TO MY WIFE TERESA FIELDS FOR HER DISPOSAL IF SHE WISHES OR IF SHE DOES NOT SURVIVE ME THE ASHES SHOULD BE GIVEN TO MY NEPHEW VICTOR PALMERI FOR HIS DISPOSAL

Mr Sydney H Fields
172 Central Park W Apt 20?
New York, NY 10025-8213

212-678-1494

App.147a

LAST WILL AND TESTAMENT OF SYDNEY H. FIELDS (OCTOBER 6, 2014)

I, SYDNEY H. FIELDS, residing at 372 Central Park West, Apartment 20P in the City, County and State of New York, being of sound and disposing mind and memory, do make, publish and declare this to be my Last Will and Testament, hereby revoking all prior wills and codicils made by me.

FIRST: I order and direct the payment of all my just debts and testamentary expenses as soon as practicable after my death.

SECOND: I direct that all inheritance, estate and any other tax in respect of any inheritance under this my last will and testament by reason of any State, Federal or other laws new or hereafter in force (including any interest and penalties thereon) shall be paid by my executor or alternate executor out of my residuary estate as part of the expenses of administration thereof without apportionment.

THIRD: I give and bequeath $500 to the CITY COLLEGE FUND of the CITY UNIVERSITY OF NEW YORK, $500 to the UNITED JEWISH APPEAL OF NEW YORK, and $1,000 to the BARUCH COLLEGE FUND of the CITY UNIVERSITY OF NEW YORK.

FOURTH: All the rest, residue and remainder of my property and estate, both real and personal of every kind and description and wheresoever situated which shall belong to me or be subject to my disposal at the time of my death (my residuary estate) I give and bequeath as follows:

A. 20% (twenty percent) to OLGA PALMERI, currently residing at 80 Forest Avenue, Paramus, NJ 07652. If she should predecease me, I leave her share of my residuary estate to VICTOR PALMERI, Sr.

B. 35% (thirty-five percent) to DIANA PALMERI, currently residing at 750 Ridgewood Avenue, Oradel, NJ 07649. If she should predecease me, I leave her share in equal percentages to her husband, DAVID and each of their three children, with DAVID to act as Trustee of the shares left to their children until they reach majority.

C. 20% (twenty percent) to VICTOR PALMERI, Jr., currently residing at 80 Forest Avenue, Paramus NJ 07652. If he should predecease me, I leave his share to OLGA PALMERI.

D. 15% (fifteen percent) to CYNTHIA PALMERI, currently residing at 80 Forest Avenue, Paramus NJ 07652. If she should predecease me, I leave her share in equal shares to each of her children, per stirpes.

E. 10% (ten percent) to ANA MARIA GARZON YEPEZ, currently residing at Francisco Oliva Oe3-73 y Cap. Edmundo Chiriboga Casa #46, Quito, Ecuador, or her heirs if she should predecease me.

FIFTH:

(a) Because my son Kenneth L. Fields refused to let me visit my grandchildren, Elizabeth and Alex P. Fields and refused to have a relationship with me even after a lawsuit where I sought visitation rights, I deliberately make no provision for him in this Will and it is my intention that he receive no part of my estate.

(b) Because my son Richard Fields hired a lawyer to sue me for money and because I had to have him arrested and brought to court for harassment of me and my wife, Teresa I deliberately make no provision for him in this Will and it is my intention that he receive no part of my estate.

(c) Because my grandchildren Elizabeth Fields, Lewis D. Fields and Alex P. Fields refused to have a relationship with me after reaching adulthood, I deliberately make no provision for them in this Will and it is my intention that they not receive any part of my estate.

SIXTH: I hereby nominate constitute and appoint my niece DIANA PALMERI, executor of this my Last Will and Testament and I direct that no bond or other security shall be required of her (or any alternate executor hereunder) for the faithful performance of her fiduciary duties hereunder in any jurisdiction.

In the event that my niece DIANA PALMERI shall predecease me, or if she is unwilling or unable to serve as my executor for any reason whatsoever then I nominate constitute and appoint VICTOR PALMIERI, Sr. as alternate executor with like powers and immunities.

In addition to the powers and authority conferred on executors by law, and to enable my executor or alternate executor to liquidate and distribute my estate in a prompt and orderly manner, I authorize and empower my executor and alternate executor to

App.150a

do everything she or he deems necessary or desirable for the proper execution or discharge of any powers or duties held by or imposed on her by this will or by applicable law, even though it would not be authorized or appropriate for fiduciaries under any statute or rule of law, including the power to maintain, sell, pledge mortgage, lease transfer, exchange, convert or otherwise dispose of any property in my estate, to make sales publicly or privately wholly or partly on credit, delegate discretionary powers to agents, remunerate them and pay their expenses, distribute in kind or in money or partly to each compromise or otherwise adjust any claims or demands in favor of or against my estate, and to execute and deliver such instruments as may be necessary to carry out any of these powers, subject only to the duty to act in good faith and with responsible care.

SEVENTH: It is my wish to take full advantage of the unified credit and state death tax credit available to my estate (provided the use of such credit does not require an increase in the state death taxes payable) but no other credit, and after taking into account property disposed of by this will and property passing outside of this will which is includable in my gross estate and does not qualify for the marital or charitable deduction.

EIGHTH: If any beneficiary hereunder shall in any manner directly or indirectly, attempt to contest or oppose the validity of this will or commence, maintain or join in (except as a party defendant), or be in any way directly or indirectly interested or instrumental in the institution or maintenance of any action or proceeding in any court for the purpose of preventing the probate of this will or for the purpose of attacking the

App.151a

validity of this will or any provision hereof, then in such event such beneficiary shall forfeit his or her share hereunder, all provisions in this will for the benefit of such contesting beneficiary shall be revoked, such contesting beneficiary and his or her descendants shall be deemed to have predeceased me and shall receive no part of my estate in intestacy or otherwise and all such benefits shall be disposed of as part of my residuary estate except to the extent such contesting beneficiary is a beneficiary of a share of my residuary estate, in which event such share shall be forfeited and apportioned pro rata among other beneficiaries sharing in my residuary estate.

NINTH: It is my wish that upon my death, my body be buried in the YCFC family plot at Beth David Cemetery in Queens, New York.

IN WITNESS WHEREOF, I have subscribed and sealed and do publish and declare these presents as and for my Last Will and Testament, in the presence of the witnesses attesting the same at my request, this 6th day of October, 2014.

/s/ Sydney H. Fields (L.S.)

On this 6th day of October, 2014, SYDNEY H. FIELDS, the above-named Testator, in our presence subscribed and sealed the foregoing instrument and declared the same to be her Last Will and Testament; and we, thereupon, at her request and in her presence and in the presence of each other, have hereunto subscribed our names as attesting witnesses.

App.152a

/s/ Jill Curtin
220 West 71st Street
New York, NY 10023

/s/ Susan Lehman
220 W. 71st St. 1132
New York, NY 10023

App.153a

AFFIDAVIT OF JILL CURTIN

State of New York
County of New York

Each of the undersigned, being duly sworn, deposes and say:

The within Will was subscribed at the end thereof by SYDNEY H. FIELDS, the within named Testator, in the presence of the undersigned, on the 6th day of ~~July 2006~~, October 2014, at the Law Offices of Edward R. Curtin, 220 West 71st Street, New York, NY 10023. Said Testator at the time of making such subscription declared the instrument so subscribed to be his Last Will and Testament.

Each of the undersigned thereupon signed his or her name as a witness at the end of said Will, at the request of said Testator and in his presence and sight and in the presence and sight of each other. Said Testator was, at the time of so executing said Will, over the age of 18 years and, in the respective opinions of the undersigned, of sound mind, memory and understanding and not under any restraint or in any respect incompetent to make a Will.

The Testator, in the respective opinions of the undersigned, could read, write and converse in the English language and was suffering from no defect of sight, hearing or speech, or from any other physical or mental impairment which would affect his capacity to make a valid Will. This Will was executed as a single, original instrument and was not executed in counterparts.

Each of the undersigned was acquainted with said Testator at such time and makes this affidavit at his

App.154a

request. The within Will was shown to the undersigned at the time this affidavit was made, and was examined by each of them as to the signature of said Testator and of the undersigned. The foregoing instrument was executed by said Testator and witnessed by each of the undersigned affiants under the supervision of Edward R. Curtin, an attorney at-law.

/s/ Jill Curtin

/s/ Susan Lehman

Sworn to before me this 6th day of October, 2014

/s/ Edward R. Curtin
Notary Public, State of New York
No. 02CU5015786
Qualified in New York County
Commission Expires July 26, 2016

App.155a

AFFIDAVIT

STATE OF NEW YORK   )
) ss.:
COUNTY OF NEW YORK)

Each of the undersigned, being duly sworn, deposes and say:

The within Will was subscribed at the end thereof by SYDNEY H. FIELDS, the within named Testator, in the presence of the undersigned, on the __ day of July, 2006, at the Law Offices of Edward R. Curtin, 220 West 71st Street, New York, NY 10023. Said Testator at the time of making such subscription declared the instrument so subscribed to be his Last Will and Testament.

Each of the undersigned thereupon signed his or her name as a witness at the end of said Will, at the request of said Testator and in his presence and sight and in the presence and sight of each other. Said Testator was, at the time of so executing said Will, over the age of 18 years and, in the respective opinions of the undersigned, of sound mind, memory and understanding and not under any restraint or in any respect incompetent to make a Will.

Erca
October,
2014

The Testator, in the respective opinions of the undersigned, could read, write and converse in the English language and was suffering from no defect of sight, hearing or speech, or from any other physical or mental impairment which would affect his capacity to make a valid Will. This Will was executed as a single, original instrument and was not executed in counterparts.

Each of the undersigned was acquainted with said Testator at such time and makes this affidavit at his request. The within Will was shown to the undersigned at the time this affidavit was made, and was examined by each of them as to the signature of said Testator and of the undersigned. The foregoing instrument was executed by said Testator and witnessed by each of the undersigned affiants under the supervision of Edward R. Curtin, an attorney-at-law.

Sworn to before me this
6th day of October, 2014

Notary Public

EDWARD R. CURTIN
Notary Public, State of New York
No. 02CU6015786
Qualified in New York County
Commission Expires July 26, 2016

DATE
WAS
CHANGED

App.157a

APPENDIX: G
CREDIBILITY OF RESPONDENT AND HER LAWYERS

App.158a

AFFIRMATION IN SUPPORT OF MOTION FOR SUMMARY JUDGMENT (APRIL 19, 2016)

SURROGATE'S COURT OF THE STATE OF NEW YORK, COUNTY OF NEW YORK

PROBATE PROCEEDING
SYDNEY H. FIELDS,

Deceased.

File No. 2016-111

Edward R. Curtin, an attorney-at-law duly admitted to practice law before the courts of the State of New York, hereby affirms the following under penalty of perjury:

I am the attorney for the Estate of Sydney H. Fields, deceased. I make this affirmation in support of the Petitioner's Summary Judgment Motion to dismiss the Objections to Probate filed by Richard Fields in this proceeding and to admit the Last Will and Testament of Sydney H. Fields dated October 6, 2014 the "Will"). An analysis of each of the allegations made by attorney Dehai Zhang on information and belief reveals that each of them are without basis in fact and are totally devoid of merit, and should be dismissed:

App.159a

1. **"That the Alleged Will Was Not Duly Executed in Accordance with the Law of the State of New York"**

The requirements for due execution of a will are clearly articulated in EPTL § 3-21. To establish due execution, a proponent must show that: (i) the testator's signature is present at the end of the instrument; (ii) the testator has signed the instrument in the presence of at least two attesting witnesses, (iii) the testator declared to each of the attesting witnesses that the instrument was his will; and (iv) the witnesses signed the instrument at the testator's request.

Annexed as Exhibit A hereto is a true copy of the Will, including the Affidavit of the attesting witnesses, which on its face satisfies each and every requirement specified in EPTL § 3-2.1 for due execution of a will.

2. **"That SYDNEY H. FIELDS, Was Not Competent on October 6, 2014 to Make a Will, in that He Lacked Testamentary Capacity"**

The allegation on information and belief that Sydney H. Fields "lacked testamentary capacity" is absolutely refuted by the sworn affidavit of the two witnesses who were present at the signing of the Will, each stating that Mr. Fields was "in the respective opinions of the undersigned, of sound mind, memory and understanding and not under any restraint or in any respect incompetent to make a valid Will." As the supervising attorney who drafted the Will and supervised the execution thereof, I attest and affirm without qualification that Sydney Fields was completely competent, lucid and keenly aware of the contents of the Will and the dispositions made therein. In fact, the Will was drawn and executed in October of 2014 to replace and supersede a will which he had executed on July 28, 2006, a true copy of which is annexed hereto as Exhibit B. In the previous, superseded will, Mr. Fields' had left the bulk of his estate to his wife Teresa Fields, but when she died in September of 2014, Mr. Fields was compelled to have a new Will drafted, wherein he provided for his residuary estate to be distributed amongst members of his deceased wife's family, whom he had come to embrace as his own family. Thus, he contacted me, told me the changes he wanted to make, and arranged to come to my law office to execute the revised Will in front of two witnesses. All of the substantive changes were provided to me by Sydney H. Fields, and by him alone. What was not changed in the October 6, 2014 Will, was the following provision:

> "FIFTH: (b) Because my son Richard Fields hired a lawyer to sue me for money and because I had to have him arrested and brought to court for harassment of me and my wife, Teresa I deliberately make no provision for him in this Will and it is my intention that he receive no part of my estate."

In fact, prior to the execution of the Will, Mr. Fields told me to make sure that this provision remained in the Will, and I read this provision to him along with the other provisions of the Will to assure him that it was still in his Will prior to his execution thereof.

App.161a

3. "That the Aforesaid Alleged Will Is Not the Last Will and Testament of SYDNEY H. FIELDS, in That the Subscription and Publication Thereof, If in Fact It Was Subscribed and Published by SYDNEY H. FIELDS, Was a Mistake in That He Did Not Know and Understand Its Contents"

There is simply no factual basis for this allegation. It was Sydney H. Fields who initiated the drafting of the Will to replace the July 28, 2006 will after the death of his wife Teresa, and it was Sydney H. Fields who told me what he wanted the Will to provide and how his estate was to be distributed among the beneficiaries named therein. He was intimately familiar with all of the provisions of the Will, and fully understood its contents. Moreover, the provision of the Will which is the obvious reason and basis for Objectant's filing of his objections (Article FIFTH, (b) "Because my son Richard Fields hired a lawyer to sue me for money and because I had to have him arrested and brought to court for harassment of me and my wife, Teresa I deliberately make no provision for him in this Will and it is my intention that he receive no part of my estate.") already existed in the July 28, 2006 will of Sydney H. Fields which he authored and subscribed to, and was reiterated verbatim in the October 6, 2014 Will at the express direction of the Testator.

App.162a

4. "That the Aforesaid Alleged Will Was Not in Its Entirety Freely and Voluntarily Executed by SYDNEY H. FIELDS Because the Aforesaid Alleged Will Was Prepared and Obtained and the Subscription and Publication Thereof Were Procured, If in Fact It Was Subscribed and Published by SYDNEY H. FIELDS, by Fraud, Duress and Undue Influence Practiced on the Late SYDNEY H. FIELDS by OLGA PALMERI. VICTOR PALMERI, SR., DIANA PALMERI, DAVID PALMERI, VICTOR PALMERI, JR., CYNTHIA PALMERI AND ANA MARIA GARZON YEPEZ, WHO ACTED IN CONCERT WITH EACH OTHER, INDEPENDENTLY, OR BOTH"

As previously stated, the provision of the Will cited above (Article FIFTH, (b) "Because my son Richard Fields hired a lawyer to sue me for money and because I had to have him arrested and brought to court for harassment of me and my wife, Teresa I deliberately make no provision for him in this Will and it is my intention that he receive no part of my estate.") was initially authored and subscribed to by the Testator in his July 28, 2006 Last Will & Testament), and was expressly restated verbatim in the Will now being challenged by Objectant. The harassment referred to by Sydney Fields in his Will includes, inter alia, certain threatening and menacing photographs of Objectant wielding lethal weapons which Objectant sent to Sydney Fields and his wife Teresa (see Exhibit C hereto), and the unlawful obtaining of Sydney Fields' tax records from the U.S. Internal Revenue Service by Objectant by forging Sydney Fields' signature (see Exhibit D hereto). On several occasions, Sydney H. Fields was compelled to seek and

App.163a

obtain Orders of Protection against Objectant Richard Fields from the New York City Criminal Court and New York County Family Court (see Exhibit E hereto).

The threatening harassment of Sydney Fields and his wife Teresa by Objectant Richard Fields which caused Sydney Fields to seek and obtain Orders of Protections against Richard Fields, and the forged obtaining of tax information by Objectant, were personal to Sydney Fields and his wife Teresa, and understandably motivated Sydney to exclude Richard Fields from receiving any bequest under his Will. This was clearly not due to "fraud, duress and undue influence practiced on the late SYDNEY H FIELDS by OLGA PALMERI, VICTOR PALMERI, SR., DIANA PALMERI, DAVID PALMERI, VICTOR PALMERI, JR, CYNTHIA PALMERI AND ANA MARIA GARZON YEPEZ, WHO ACTED IN CONCERT WITH EACH OTHER, INDEPENDENTLY, OR BOTH." as alleged by Objectant herein. None of said individuals were the target of Objectant's threats and harassment, so there would be no logical reason for any of them to practice fraud, duress or undue influence on the late Sydney H. Fields to not leave anything to Richard Fields in his Will. It is a boilerplate objection without any substance or basis in fact and which runs contrary to the facts of this case, and as such should be summarily rejected by this Court.

/s/ Edward R. Curtin

Dated: New York, New York
April 19, 2016

App.164a

LETTER FROM MARTIN TO LAUBSCHER (MARCH 27, 2017)

JULES MARTIN HAAS
ATTORNEY AT LAW
845 Third Avenue Suite 1400, New York, NY 10022
Tel: (212) 355-2575 Fax: (112) 751-5911
attorney.haas845(a)gmail.com

By Hand

Surrogate Rita Mella
New York County Surrogate's Court
31 Chambers Street, Room 401
New York, NY 10007
Attn: Jay C. Laubscher, Court Referee

RE: Estate of Sydney Fields, Deceased
File No.: 2016-111

Dear Mr. Laubscher:

I along with Edward Curtin, Esq. and Novick & Associates represent Diana Palmeri, the petitioner herein and the preliminary executor of the above estate.

I am writing to the Court to obtain an immediate emergency conference with the Court regarding this proceeding. Objectant is a son of the decedent and is represented by Richard A. Chen, Esq., with an office located at 41-60 Main Street, Suite 203, Flushing, New York 11355. The need for an emergency conference is two-fold. First and foremost, Objectant has been incessantly mailing inflammatory and threatening correspondence to co-counsel, Edward Curtin, Esq. Annexed hereto as Exhibit A are copies of a few of the letters

App.165a

which Objectant has recently sent to Mr. Curtin. Some of the letters have included assertions by Objectant that he does not want to pursue this proceeding.

Mr. Curtin has received letters from Objectant on March 13, 2017, March 15, 2017 (12 letters), March 16, 2017 (15 letters), March 17, 2017 (13 letters), March 18, 2017 (9 letters), March 20, 2017 (14 envelopes containing numerous letters) and on other dates thereafter and most recently today (March 27, 2017).

On Monday, March 20, 2017, Objectant telephoned Mr. Curtin at his office. Mr. Curtin immediately advised Objectant that he (Mr. Curtin) would not speak with Objectant and Objectant hung-up the telephone.

Mr. Curtin was the attorney draftsperson of the decedent's Last Will dated October 6, 2014 as well as prior Wills of the decedent. Additionally, Mr. Curtin was the attorney who supervised the execution of the October 6, 2014 Will. Mr. Curtin's deposition was conducted on February 1, 2017. Petitioner expects to rely on Mr. Curtin's testimony in support of the probate of the decedent's Will.

As can be seen from Exhibit A, the aforementioned letters sent to Mr. Curtin by Objectant contain statements regarding Objectant's involvement with weapons, explosives and direct threats made by Objectant to the decedent, as well as other improper and invasion of privacy conduct in which Objectant asserts to have engaged in. Equally disturbing are Objectant's statements which appear to be best suited by being directed to and discussed with his own attorney, Richard Chen, Esq.

Mr. Chen was sent copies of Objectant's letters on March 16, 17 and 21, 2017. On March 23, 2017 I

App.166a

emailed a letter to Mr. Chen (Exhibit B). On March 23, 2017, I received Mr. Chen's response to my letter (Exhibit C). I then responded to Mr. Chen on March 23, 2017 and requested a response from Mr. Chen by the close of business on Monday, March 27, 2017. (Exhibit D). No response has been received.

While the gross impropriety of Objectant directing correspondence directly to Mr. Curtin is apparent, the implicit threats and sinister nature of the letters is chilling and shocking.

In view of the severe, ominous and improper character of the communications directed towards Mr. Curtin, which is implicitly directed towards petitioner, petitioner requests immediate Court intervention.

The additional need for a conference relates to the ongoing discovery in this proceeding. Objectant's deposition was begun on February 24, 2017 but not yet completed. The examination was scheduled to resume at the Courthouse on Friday, March 24, 2017. However, as stated in Mr. Chen's letter of March 23, 2017, Objectant's continued deposition was cancelled and has not been re-scheduled. The most recent Stipulation of the parties that was filed with this Court sets forth March 31, 2017 as the date for completion of Objectant's deposition. (Exhibit E). It is apparent that the discovery schedule will need to be extended.

During Objectant's initial deposition, Objectant related that he was presently taking psychotropic drugs and that the medication might affect his ability to answer questions and recall events. Objectant testified that he is a diagnosed paranoid schizophrenic.

I wish to stress that the purpose of this application for an emergency conference is to obtain Court inter-

App.167a

vention in a situation that is clearly beyond the control of petitioner's counsel and is affecting the appropriate procedures to be followed in this matter. Clearly, petitioner and her counsel and potential witnesses cannot and should not be subjected to abusive and uncontrolled conduct by Objectant of any sort and certainly that which contains blatant references to physical and personal harm.

There are additional discovery issues to be discussed as well, unrelated to Objectant's conduct.

In view of the above, it is requested that the Court schedule an emergency conference to discuss the above matter.

Respectfully,

/s/ Jules Martin Haas, Esq.

JMH/sb
enc.

cc: Richard Chen, Esq. (Via email)
Attorney for Objectant, Richard Fields

Edward Curtin, Esq. (Via email)
Co-Counsel for Diana Palmeri

Albert Messina, Esq. (Via email)
Novick & Associates
Co-Counsel for Diana Palmeri

App.168a

LETTER FROM DR. MIHAILESCU AND DR. GIOVE (APRIL 16, 2019)

THE BROOKDALE UNIVERSITY HOSPITAL
AND MEDICAL CENTER
One Brookdale Plaza
Brooklyn. N.Y. 1 121 2-3198
(718) 240-5000 * Fax (718) 240-5451
brookdalchospital.org

04/16/19

To whom it may concern:

Mr. Fields, Richard (DOB 02/06/1963) was hospitalized at Brookdale University Hospital from admission date 03/20/19 to discharge date 04/16/19.

Sincerely,

/s/ Vivian Mihailescu, MD

/s/ AnnMarie Give, MSW

App.169a

Search Results

- Vivian G. Mihailescu Reviews |Brooklyn, NY | Vitals.com
  https://www.vitals.com/doctors/Dr_Vivian_Mihailescu.html
    Rating: 5-1 vote

    Vivian G. Mihailescu is a Doctor primarily located in Brooklyn, NY with another office in Brooklyn, NY. Her specialties include Psychiatry. She speaks English.

- Dr. Vivian Mihailescu, MD–Brooklyn, NY | Psychiatry–Doximity
  https://www.doximity.com > States > New York > Brooklyn

    Dr. Vivian Mihailescu, MD is a board certified psychiatrist in Brooklyn, New York. She is affiliated with Brookdale Hospital Medical Center.

- Dr. Vivian G. Mihailescu, MD, Brooklyn, NY (11212) Psychiatrist Reviews
  https://www.zocdoc.com > Find a Psychiatrist

    Book an appointment online now with Dr. Vivian G Mihailescu, MD or Brooklyn, NY (11212). Read verified patient reviews and make an appointment instantly.

- Dr. Vivian G. Mihailescu-Psychiatry, Brooklyn NY
  https://www.healthcare4ppl.com/physician/new . . /vivian-g-mihailescu-1326013681.ht . . .

    Dr. Vivian G. Mihailescu is a Psychiatry Specialist in Brooklyn, New York. She graduated with honors in 1986. Having more than 33 years of diverse experiences. . . .

App.170a

APPENDIX: H
THE FAMILY HISTORY OF SYDNEY FIELDS

App.171a

LETTER FROM ATTORNEY MESSINA TO ATTORNEY CHEN (APRIL 16, 2019)

Novick & Associates
Attorneys at Law
202 East Main Street
Huntington, New York 11743
Telephone (631) 547-0300
Facsimile (631) 547-0212

April 24, 2018

Richard Alan Chen, Esq.
41-60 Main Street, Suite 203
Flushing, New York 11355

                Re: Estate of Sydney Fields
                File No. 2016-111

Dear Mr. Chen:

    We received the enclosed documents from your client, who claims that he is pro se. Since we have not received a consent to change attorneys for matters before the Surrogate's Court we are addressing this matter to you.

    The enclosed documents are hereby rejected and are being returned to Objectants' counsel for non-compliance with the CPLR.

                            Very truly yours

                            /s/ Albert V. Messina, Jr.

App.172a

OPINION OF THE SUPERIOR COURT OF NEW JERSEY, CHANCERY DIVISION (MAY 14, 1998)

SUPERIOR COURT OF NEW JERSEY
CHANCERY DIVISION-FAMILY PART
MERCER COUNTY

SYDNEY H. FIELDS,

Plaintiff,

v.

KENNETH L. FIELDS and
ALICE PRESTON, His Wife,

Defendants.

Docket No.: FD 11 913 98

Before: DELEHEY, J.S.C.

DELEHEY, J.S.C.

Plaintiff, Sydney H. Fields, ("Sydney"), age 79, is the paternal grandfather of Elizabeth Fields, age 15, and Alexander Preston Fields, age 12. Sydney lives with his wife Teresa in New York City. Defendant, Kenneth L. Fields ("Kenneth"), age 52, is Sydney's son. He and his wife, Alice Preston, are the parents of Elizabeth and Alexander with whom they live in Princeton, New Jersey. Sydney, who has not seen his grandchildren since 1992, seeks visitation with

App.173a

Elizabeth and Alexander under the New Jersey Grandparents Visitation Statute, N.J.S.A. 9:2-7.1.

Trial was conducted on March 3, 1998. The testimony and evidence presented essentially mirrored briefs submitted in advance of and at the conclusion of trial. Sydney Fields, Dr. Mathias Hagovsky, Kenneth L. Fields, Alice Preston, Betsy Fields and Alexander Fields testified.

Findings of Fact and Conclusions of Law

Sydney married Sarah Fields, Kenneth's mother, in 1943. When Kenneth was three years old, his mother, Sarah, became mentally ill and was institutionalized, leaving Kenneth to be reared primarily by Sydney's mother. In 1957, Sydney obtained an annulment of his marriage to Sarah Fields. In 1960 he married Gladys Fields. A son, Richard Fields, Kenneth's half brother, was born in 1963, when Kenneth was seventeen years of age. In 1969 Sydney divorced Gladys, who was mentally unstable.

Kenneth and Gladys did not get along. Sydney concedes that "Gladys was a cruel person. I was caught in the middle. I had a young baby. I felt sorry for Ken. Ever since Richard was born Gladys was cruel to Ken." In 1963, Kenneth entered Massachusetts Institute of Technology, Sydney paying the tuition. During his college years, Kenneth never returned to the family home. He saw Sydney in 1969, when Kenneth's grandmother died, and did not see Sydney again until 1977, when he returned from living in the West. by that time Sydney had married Teresa, a South American immigrant employed by a Catholic charitable organization.

App.174a

Elizabeth was born in 1982. Shortly thereafter, Kenneth and Alice began establishing a relationship with the grandparents that included the grandchildren, Elizabeth, and later, Alexander. Sydney and Teresa saw the grandchildren ten or twelve times per year, usually at restaurants or theaters in New York, although there were occasions when they celebrated Seders together. On occasion, Sydney and Teresa visited in Princeton, and Teresa, of Spanish descent, who was not the grandchildren's biological grandmother, acquired the name "Abuelita", a Spanish word meaning sweet grandmother. The children often corresponded with "Grandpa Syd," especially Elizabeth, enclosing compositions, class photos and greeting cards. Sydney would reply with words of praise and encouragement. The importance of the grandchildren in their lives is demonstrated by Sydney's retention of the treasured correspondence from the children, and by Teresa's occasional trips alone to visit the children in Princeton.

In 1980, Sydney, a certified public accountant since 1943, lent $83,000 to Kenneth and Alice, which enabled them to buy their home. Sydney told Kenneth to have the mortgage drawn by Kenneth's lawyer with interest at a rate of 7½% at a time when interest rates were 14%. Kenneth and Alice paid off the loan in 1992, about the same time that they severed all communications with Sydney.

Kenneth's determination to sever communications with Sydney and Teresa springs from an immediate concern for the safety of his family and from vivid recollections of an unhappy childhood and adolescence for which he holds Sydney responsible. Kenneth recalled that when he was five years old his parents separated. "My mother was crazy," mentally ill, schizophrenic.

App.175a

She was receiving shock treatments. Kenneth recalls being left in the custody of a mentally ill mother living in an apartment in Brooklyn. Sydney had left them. Eventually, a neighbor complained that Kenneth was not going to school. Shortly thereafter Sarah, his mother, was committed to the Brooklyn State Hospital. The following year Kenneth lived with seven or eight of his mother's brothers and sisters, all of whom were neurotic. Sydney then took custody of Kenneth and they lived with Sydney's mother, until Sydney married Gladys. During the years that Kenneth and Sydney resided with Kenneth's grandmother, he described his relationship with his father as "cool, good, until Syd married Gladys. I told Syd that she (Gladys) was nuts" —a prophesy which was eventually fulfilled when Sydney's marriage to Gladys ended in a 1969 divorce.

Kenneth and his half brother, Richard, are strangers to one another, having spoken to each other less than a handful of times in their entire lives. On one occasion Kenneth met Richard in New York City. He immediately told Sydney that to "save" Richard he had to get him away from Gladys.

As Ken saw it, Richard was developing into a psychopath. In the mid-1980's Kenneth, a mathematics professor, went to the Psychology Department at Rider University and described Richard to a fellow faculty member, who shared with Kenneth a chapter from a psychology text. Kenneth forwarded a copy of the text to Sydney, who refused to acknowledge Richard's schizophrenia and psychosis.

In 1989, Sydney forwarded to Kenneth a summary of Richard's threatening conduct which began in February 1989 (Exhibit D-1). The summary was accompan-

App.176a

ied by a packet of correspondence (Exhibit D-2) written by Richard to Sydney and to Sydney's brother, Sol.

The correspondence from Richard is bizarre, disturbing and blatantly scary. It reflects all of the indicia of paranoid schizophrenia—a sense of being exploited, threatening language, unforgiving grudges, conflicting emotions and disorganized, deranged thoughts. At one time, Richard left a note under the door of Sydney's apartment:

> Next time I won't leave you a note under your door at 20P. If you steal my check again I will wait for you many hours to fulfill our murder-suicide pact. Our father-son pact.
>
> Don't think a penthouse is a secure place to live. Because it is too high to let you get help in time.
>
> I didn't pay $350.00 cash to buy my gun just to let it sit home. I will use it with pleasure

On another occasion Richard wrote:

> I am Richard Jack Fields. Sydney H. Fields is my father.
>
> Kenneth Lewis Fields ruined my life!
>
> Kenneth Kenneth Kenneth Kenneth Kenneth Kenneth Kenneth Kenneth Kenneth Kenneth, [etc.]

On another occasion Richard wrote:

> Dear Uncle Sol:
>
> I just had a horrible nightmare. I just don't know why tonight I had such a disturbed sleep. I just felt I had to share the dream with

you. I was standing in a crowded classroom. There were some math equations on a blackboard. And I shot the instructor in the head in front of them. I then said to everyone: "Dad now only has one son," I looked around. Students screamed, "Dr. Fields is dead." I looked at the floor and saw Kenneth lying there and blood spilling out onto the floor. Then I woke up. I just don't know why I had such a horrible dream. Perhaps you can help explain it to me.

Another letter to Uncle Sol in March 1991:

Dear Uncle Sol:

I have an interesting story to tell you. When I went to Rider College to get Kenneth's picture, they were only selling the 1989 college yearbook. They had the 1988 yearbook, but they refused to sell it. Well, guess what I did? I bought the 1989 yearbook and waited for the clerk, who was the only one there, to go to the bathroom. When he did, I switched the 1989 yearbook with the 1988 yearbook. Do you know why? Because the 1989 yearbook did not have Kenneth's picture. The 1988 yearbook had Kenneth's picture. When the clerk came back, I don't know if he noticed it because I left in a hurry. I was waiting for the bus back to the train station within a short time. I just wanted to share that with you.

Love, Richard

App.178a

Later, Richard would write:

> My friend has advised me where Elizabeth and Alexander go to school. Please inform me if I should pay him his fee to assist Kenneth with his busy schedule by picking them up after school. He very much wishes to do so.

To Sydney he wrote:

> Those two goons I thought were working for me are really your double agents. That girl in my Central America course is also your double agent. I got myself a .22 caliber revolver for my protection. Don't send any more people to me. I will leave you alone. All I care about now is my college work.

Another Richard note:

> 114 Linden Lane
> Princeton, New Jersey
> [Kenneth and Alice's residence]
> Arson
> Bank Leumi

In December 1995, Sydney received threatening letters, photographs and weapons from Richard. He obtained from the New York Courts an Order of Protection, which applied to Teresa and himself.

In 1991, Sydney finally agreed to have Richard examined by two psychiatrists. Despite their diagnosis of schizophrenia, he would not consent to Richard's institutionalization.

App.179a

In 1991, Kenneth concluded that Richard had become his problem when Richard started writing threatening letters to him.

In May 1991, Kenneth concluded that he should sever ties with Sydney, believing that Sydney's contacts with Richard were in some way exacerbating Richard's animosity toward his family and him. Once Kenneth severed relations with Sydney "the crazy letters from Richard ceased."

Since 1992, Kenneth and Sydney have spoken only once, in 1995 after Richard was arrested on Sydney's complaint of domestic violence. As Kenneth explains it, "I would have no objection to meeting with Sydney and Teresa, if Richard were arrested. Richard is the problem!" So long as Richard remains free, Kenneth believes that the lives of his family are in jeopardy. "There is someone (Richard) out there that wants them dead." Kenneth expresses the view that it was Sydney who allowed Richard to develop into a full-blown psychopath. He fears the transmission of any information about himself or his family to Sydney. "I don't want Sydney to know the details of our personal lives. I do not trust Sydney."

Richard's conduct has challenged the security of Kenneth and Alice's very close family. The children, both of whom are exceptionally intelligent, have been made privy to Richard's writings. They are aware of his threats. Consequently, the family is more vigilant, and certain precautions, such as insuring that the children's photographs do not appear in any publications.

The New Jersey Grandparents Visitation Act provides:

App.180a

a. A grandparent or any sibling of a child residing in this State may make application before the Superior Court, in accordance with the rules of Court, for an order for visitation. It shall be the burden of the applicant to prove by a preponderance of the evidence that the granting of visitation is in the best interests of the child.

b. In making a determination on an application filed pursuant to this section, the court shall consider the following factors:

(1) The relationship between the child and the applicant;

(2) The relationship between each of the child's parents or the person with whom the child is residing and the applicant;

(3) The time which has elapsed since the child last bad contact with the applicant;

(4) The effect that such visitation will have on the relationship between the child and the child's parents or the person with whom the child is residing;

(5) If the parents are divorced or separated, the time sharing arrangement which exists between the parents with regard to the child;

(6) The good faith of the applicant in filing the application;

(7) Any history of physical, emotional or sexual abuse or neglect by the applicant; and

(8) any other factor relevant to the best interests of the child.

App.181a

c. With regard to any application made pursuant to this section, it shall be prima facie evidence that visitation is in the child's best interest if the applicant had, in the past, been a full-time caretaker for the child.

The New Jersey Grandparents Visitation Act is designed to promote relationships between grandparents and grandchildren. Ordinarily, grandparents' rights of visitation are acknowledged only where the children's family has been divided by divorce. The New Jersey law is unique in that it permits grandparents to obtain visitation, even where the grandchildren's family is intact. Therefore, in New Jersey grandparents may obtain visitation if the factors contained in the statute are satisfied. The burden of proof rests with the grandparents.

Dr. Mathias R. Hagovsky, a psychologist, who interviewed only Sydney and Teresa, expressed the view that both grandparents and grandchildren benefit from a close relationship—a view wonderfully articulated, almost poetically, by Justice Pashman in *Mimkon v. Ford*, 66 N.J. 426 (1975):

> It is biological fact that grandparents are bound to their grandchildren by the unbreakable links of heredity. It is common human experience that the concern and interest grandparents take in the welfare of their grandchildren far exceeds anything explicable in purely biological terms. A very special relationship often arises and continues between grandparents and grandchildren. The tensions and conflicts which commonly mar relations between parents and children are often absent between those very same parents

App.182a

and their grandchildren. Visits with a grandparent are often a precious part of a child's experience and there are benefits which devolve upon the grandchild from the relationship with his grandparents which he cannot derive from any other relationship. Neither the Legislature nor this Court is blind to human truths which grandparents and grandchildren have always known. *Id.* at 437.

Although the New Jersey Grandparents Visitation Statute contains seven specific factors to be considered, only factors one through four are applicable: (1) the relationship between the children and the applicant, (2) the relationship between the children's parents and the applicant, (3) the time which has elapsed since the children last had contact with the applicant, and (4) the effect that visitation will have on the relationship between the children and their parents.

Sydney's relationship with Elizabeth and Alexander terminated in 1992. Elizabeth was nine years of age, Alexander six. Elizabeth is now fifteen years of age, an exceptional student at Princeton High School articulate and straightforward. She has been apprised of Richard's threatening letters and understands that contact with Sydney is related to the threat which Richard poses. " . . . [W]hatever circumstances bring those letters to us should not exist." Elizabeth recognizes the dichotomy of contact between her paternal and maternal grandparents. She sees her maternal grandparents once or twice a year and has traveled with them on vacation. She does not see Sydney. She feels no antagonism towards Sydney but recognizes that they have grown apart. She expresses a reluctance to resume visitation " . . . of course I remember visiting with them, and we did have a relationship with them, I'm not denying that. But it was a long time ago and I've moved on. So, I'd really just as soon leave things as they are."

Alexander is now twelve years of age. He too is very intelligent and articulate. A seventh grader, his vocabulary includes the comfortable use of advanced vocabulary, such as "ironic." He is already doing calculus and his father presents him with math problems that would challenge accomplished college students. He does not have a strong recollection of time spent with his grandfather, but does recall Teresa's sixtieth birthday party at which he and Elizabeth were the only children in the room. Alexander and his father are very close. Each day they take a walk for about an hour. Like his father, he enjoys math and his free time pursuits are intellectual rather than athletic. He was unhappy that he had missed a day in school to attend court. He has an almost detached attitude about resumption of visitation with his grandparents. "I'm not sure how it would work out without interfering with my life." He said that he feels that he does not know Sydney and Teresa. Sadly, he does not anticipate or see any way that they could fit into his life.

Alice Preston, the children's mother, shares Kenneth's views. When asked by Teresa why visitation had stopped, Alice told her that Kenneth could not forgive Sydney "for letting Richard go down the tubes." Teresa's response was to send audio tapes on the subject of forgiveness.

The issue presented is whether the court should grant grandparent visitation if it will disturb a family's sense of security. Given all of the circumstances, the

App.184a

court concludes that Kenneth's fears, although they have not been realized, are indeed very real. Richard's threats cannot be ignored. The imposition of a court order forcing grandparent/ grandchild visitation will serve no purpose. The grandchildren presently feel distant or removed from Sydney, and they are very much aware of the threat with which Richard presents. Kenneth believes that Sydney's contact with Richard only serves to ignite Richard's psychosis and the threats that are directed at Kenneth, his wife and children. Kenneth notes that Richard's threats ceased once Kenneth ceased visitation between Sydney and his family. Whether there is a nexus between those events is unknown, but the coincidence must be weighed. Kenneth believes that Sydney provides to Richard information concerning Kenneth and his family to Richard, which only serves to ignite Richard's threats. Whether that is so is unknown, but Kenneth and his family sincerely believe it to be so. Thus, they believe that any contact with Sydney jeopardizes their security.

The legitimacy of Kenneth's fears is validated by Sydney's retention of Richard's psychotic writings and his decision to share them with Kenneth. Sydney's procurement of a protective order against Richard underscores Richard's potential for violence. And Richard's writings are, *per se*, evidence of a clear and present danger to Kenneth and his family.

The court will not substitute its judgment for that of Kenneth and Alice, and indirectly that of their children, to force visitation by the improvident operation of law. The court is satisfied that the statutory factors have not been met and that plaintiff has failed to establish by a preponderance of the evidence

App.185a

that the granting of visitation is in the best interests of the children. Accordingly, the court enters its own order denying plaintiff's application for visitation.

App.186a

TYPEWRITTEN NOTE

P.S. I love you very much and would not be writing to you so much if I was not very concerned about you. We would be living together if not for Teresa, like we should be. But we will be in the future, I promise you. I can't sleep at night knowing your life is in danger.

Dear Dad:

Don't go into the kitchen at the same time as Teresa. She can force your head into the oven and turn on the gas. It is a precaution you must take because you are living with such a dangerous person. Death is the usual result from this. I am only writing you to protect you from her just as I appreciate the fact that you want to protect me from Pia. We should protect each other. But don't worry. I already figured out how to kill Pia if I have to and Make it look "accidental." You should do the same thing with Teresa. I can help you plan it. Love,

Richard

(Over)

App.187a

SYDNEY FIELDS BRIEF AUTOBIOGRAPHY (TRANSLATION OF HANDWRITTEN DOCUMENT)

1) Father died before I was born 12/30/18.

2) Grew up with religious Jewish Grand Parents in a home with five aunts and uncles that were in a range of 1 to 12 years older than me.

3) Went to tuition free college at night city college of New York and graduated in 1940.

4) Married 1st time in 1943 to Ken's mother who became mentally ill in 1949 when Ken was 3 years old. My mother and I raised Ken beginning in 1951 until I married again to Richard's mother in 1960. After annulment of 1st marriage in 1957.

5) Divorced 2nd wife in 1969 who was cruel to Kenneth and a very poor mother to her own son and who is probably schizophrenic. Richard was 6 yrs age.

6) I had a poor relationship with Ken after 2nd marriage in 1960 and he left home in 1963 while attending M.I.T. for which I paid tuition and board.

7) Married present wife in 1975. We have had a good marriage all of these years with annual vacations that have taken us to all six of seven continents. We have good relations with each other's family and enjoyed best of relations with Ken, his wife and especially the grandchildren from 1982 to 1992

8) The big problems in our relationship with Ken and Family all occurred because of Richard's unsocial behavior to ken and Family and to me and Teresa.

[. . .]

App.188a

Overall—the children would get emotional and financial support from 2 loving people who miss them tremendously and give them love that would enrich their lives.

Nobody, especially children should be denied any source of healthy love since there is no such thing as too much love.

<u>END</u>

App.189a

PHOTOS

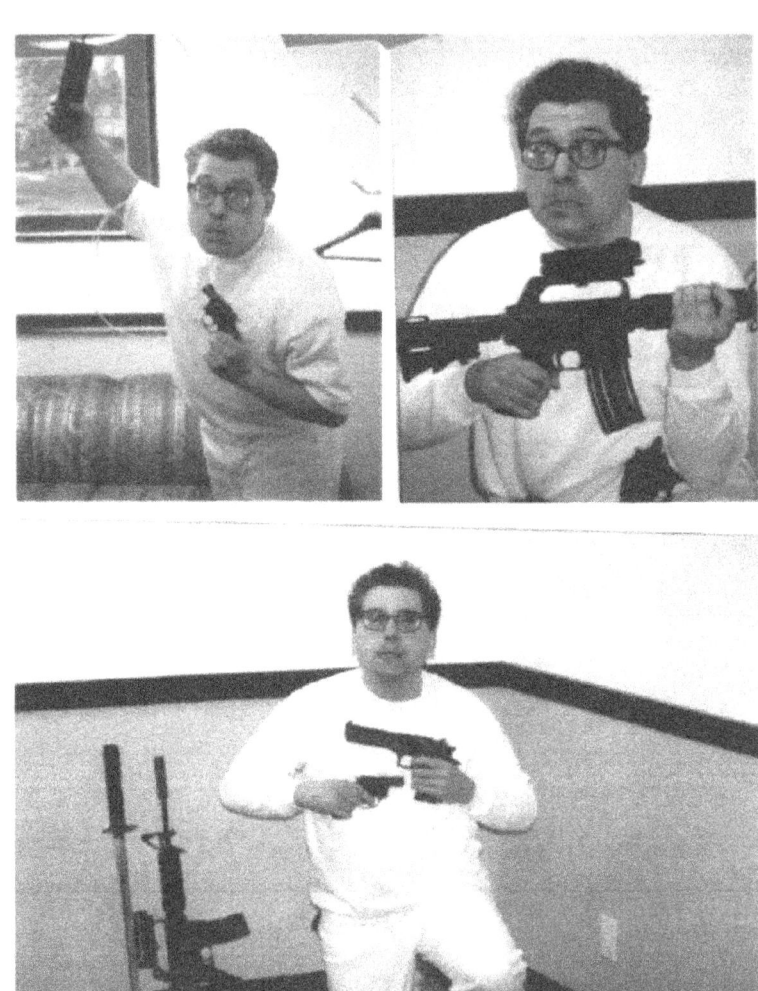

App.190a

App.191a

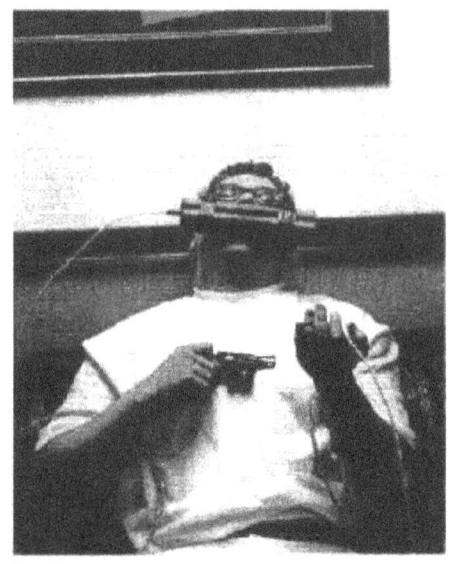

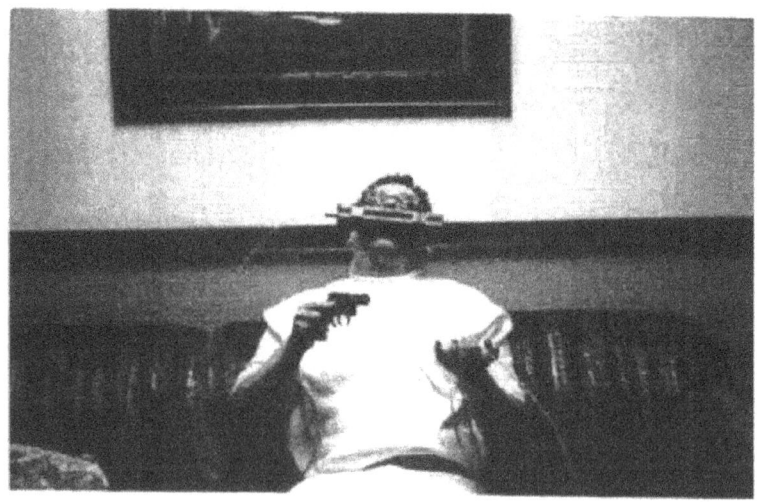

App.192a

TPO ORDER
(MARCH 18, 1996)

District Attorney of the County of New York
One Hogan Place, New York, N.Y. 10013
(212) 335-9000

Robert M. Morgenthau
District Attorney

Sydney Fields
372 Central Park West
New York, NY 10025

> RE: Temporary order of Protection
> *People v. Richard F. Fields*
> Docket No. 95N098870
> Expiration Date: 04/11/96

Dear Sydney Fields:

Enclosed please find a copy of the Temporary Order of Protection which the court issued in the above captioned criminal case. The conditions that the defendant must comply with are described in the court order. It is important that you refer to the order for the specific conditions applicable to this case.

If the defendant violates the conditions of this court order you should immediately report the incident to the police and inform them that you are in possession of an order of protection. A violation of this order may be the basis for the police officer to arrest the defendant.

To renew the Order of Protection, you must call the Witness Aid Services Unit at (212) 335-9040 at

App.193a

least one day prior to the expiration date stated above. You should also contact the Unit if you have a change of address or any questions regarding the Order.

Also, enclosed please find a pamphlet describing the services provided by our unit. If you are in need of any of these services, feel free to call the appropriate telephone number listed in the pamphlet.

                Sincerely,

                /s/ Thomas Alessandro
                Director
                Witness Aid Services Unit

App.194a

TPO ORDER
(APRIL 16, 1996)

DISTRICT ATTORNEY OF THE COUNTY OF NEW YORK
One Hogan Place, New York, N.Y. 10013
(212) 335-9000

Robert M. Morgenthau
District Attorney

Sydney Fields
372 Central Park West
New York, NY 10025

> RE: Temporary order of Protection
> *People v. Richard F. Fields*
> Docket No. 95N098870
> Expiration Date: 05/29/96

Dear Sydney Fields:

Enclosed please find a copy of the Temporary Order of Protection which the court issued in the above captioned criminal case. The conditions that the defendant must comply with are described in the court order. It is important that you refer to the order for the specific conditions applicable to this case.

If the defendant violates the conditions of this court order you should immediately report the incident to the police and inform them that you are in possession of an order of protection. A violation of this order may be the basis for the police officer to arrest the defendant.

To renew the Order of Protection, you must call the Witness Aid Services Unit at (212) 335-9040 at

App.195a

least one day prior to the expiration date stated above. You should also contact the Unit if you have a change of address or any questions regarding the Order.

                Sincerely,

                /s/ Thomas Alessandro
                Director
                Witness Aid Services Unit

App.196a

FAMILY PHOTO

1990 with Wife and Son

POSTSCRIPT

A complain to the New York State Commission on Judicial Conduct.

In July 2020, we complained about Judge Mella's decision to the New York State Commission on Judicial Conduct. The Commission is an independent agency created by the New York State Constitution to investigate complaints against New York judges.

Their website has a clear definition about a judge's misconduct. It includes: did not allow you to speak; ignored your arguments or had a connection with petitioners in the process. We therefore pointed out Judge Rita Mella's misconduct which related to ignoring important facts as below:

1. She ignored Sydney Fields' statement (was recorded by Vanguard) about that he could not read words on paper (App 56a)
2. She ignored a medical report (dated one month after the will was signed) about Sydney's both eyes were already blind. (App 43a) At the hearing, she even stopped the petitioners' lawyers from discussing Sydney's vision issue (App 28a line 15)
3. She ignored what the law requires that the executor must read the will aloud in front of a blind testator and two witnesses. Even though Curtin admitted that he never did it for Sydney (App 86a) Judge Mella still considered his will execution was duly.
4. She ignored the forgery in the instrument which listed the provisions of the will. That instrument was impossible to be written by a 96 years old blind man who could hardly control his pen. (App 122a & 123a) Without a tape record, Curtin claimed that he received it from "only Sydney".
5. She ignored a forger initials. That initial can alter the whole will by simply substituting a page which contained the will provisions. (App 18a). Mella's reason was: "there is no requirement that a testator initial the pages of a will for it to be valid"
6. She ignored our argument about it was the beneficiaries not an aide who took the blind testator to sign the will. The will put down as the beneficiary Ana Maria Garzon Yepez who lives at **Francisco Oliva Oe3-73 y Cap, Edmundo Chiriboga Casa # 46, Quito, Ecuador. (App 148a)**. That address was never shown in previous wills. Without the beneficiary being involved how come the 96 years old blind testator remembered and repeated such information to Curtin? Curtin and his witnesses can never describe the aide's age and skin color because there was no such person. Malla ignored the fact and said the aide

was sitting in a separate waiting area. However, Curtin's office was at his Manhattan home in an apartment where he has only two bedrooms, one living room and no separate waiting area.

7. She ignored the appellant's schizophrenia that made the Fields' family fall apart for years.

(App 166a, App 172a-185a) She allowed six people to receive Sydney Fields' ten-million-dollar estate because she accepted Curtin's sworn statement that Sydney considered the Palmeris as his family members. Mella ignored the fact that during the hearing, Curtin dismissed his affidavit in which he had all his sworn statements. Her decision was exactly based on those sworn statements. Below is what they said when they dismissed the affidavit:

"The April 2016 report (App. 158a) was disclosed during discovery; however, counsel did not submit the April 2016 report in opposition to the Motion for Summary Judgment. He decided, for some reason now to submit it one day before oral argument. So based on that, we have not had an opportunity to respond to the April 2016 report. We ask that your Honor reject the submission."

Actually how an affidavit was mentioned by a counsel has nothing to do with the truth or falsity of that affidavit. Its testator could make further explanation but can never dismiss it. During the appeal process they simply dismissed the affidavit and "no substitute document was issued". In that affidavit Curtin had sworn about why Sydney distributed all his assets to the Palmeri family. Judge Mella's decisions were obviously based on a dismissed affidavit with perjuries. Mella and our courts let those thieves go.

We also complained about those lawyers' misconduct to the related commission. Our complaint to the NYS Commission on Judicial Conduct was mailed in 7/18/20 and had a returning receipt with a signature. We got no response from both places up to April, 2021. In Dec 2020 I wrote a letter to follow things up:

> *To whom it may concern:*
>
> *My name is Pia Fields. In July 2020, we complained about Judge Rita Mella's misconduct related to the estate of Sydney Fields. We had a return receipt with your signature and we heard nothing from you as of Dec. 2021. Appellant Richard Fields' illness is getting worse, he did not talk to anybody for many days.*
>
> *Richard has a high IQ, he once was the New York City junior high school chess champion. He finished college with good grades but is autistic. He acted like a child without common sense when he deal with people and had a no bit of affection even to his family members. He should have had a normal life if he had enough concern from his parents. Unfortunately, his mother used him as a weapon when she was forced to divorce his father and he was harassed in school. He had to accept psychiatric treatment under court order for many years. All his life he got no job and hopes can have some money from his father. To make him feel better I spent one hundred thousand dollars to fight against that "Will" and we were mistreated by judges in our courts.*

I recall his family's history: On Dec 30, 1918 a death and a birth certificate were signed one day apart by doctor Groginsky. He, risking his life, failed to save a young father (Samuel Fishman) from the Spanish flu but successfully delivered a new born baby, Sidney Fishman (Fields). Knowing how sad it is without a father, Sydney worked very hard for his family and children. He accumulated ten million dollars in assets and still he could not raise the family up like what he hoped. When my son was born I noticed the deep affection Sydney had to his grandchild. It was sad that watching Diana Palmeri, back up by three lawyers, step on Richard and stole all Sydney's money. I can do nothing but admit that justice is not always somewhere even in the United States. Our legal enforcers prefer to do nothing besides protecting themselves. That is why so many Americans protest in the street and tear this country apart.

I hope to change the ugly ending of this case. I keep appealing and complaining. I heard nothing from you and I added this complaint along with this letter to my book "An appeal to U.S Supreme Court and a Proposal to Our President". No response is a response. People at least can see: how do law enforcers take no actions after making a beautiful speech. A postscript related to yours will make the ending of this story more interesting. In the last few years I have hung around in five courts plus two commissions.

According to your introduction: The Commission on Judicial Conduct has eleven members and meets several times a year to make decisions. It stated that "no complaint may be dismissed, no investigation may be commenced and no formal charges may be filed by staff without the commission's authorization.

However, you also make it clear that it "cannot reverse a court decision or order a new trial". That means even though you notice a judge's misconduct you will not change anything. Again, your guys maintain the law enforcers' dignity more than maintain the dignity of our laws. I carry no hope but just hanging around.

It looks like no matter how hard I complain this case will still end up in an ugly way. Never mind that I have started a new chapter, published this case and my proposals in the world. I have already translated its major content into Chinese and will contact publishers in China as well. I also attach my proposals about cutting the trade and government deficit for the world. I will promote those proposals along with the Fields' case for the rest of my life. I feel proud that as a seventy-year-old lady I am still fighting for justice for a true and better world.

A letter to the Chinese Consulate and Chinese Leaders

To the person who is in charge of publicity:

My name is Pia Fields (陈璧华), and I resided in New York City for 38 years. I am here to recommend you two books: "Why Life Events are Predestined and How Our Universe Originated" (人生为甚么注定，宇宙怎样形成) (An Appeal to the U.S Supreme Court and A Proposal to Our President " （"向美国最高法院的诉讼以及对美国总统的提议""). Both books are available in Amazon.

I try to get your attention because there are interesting content and concepts in these two books. They will increase the reputation for Chinese Culture and promote the socialist ideology CCP has. I, stand on your side, hope to reduce the capitalism's influence in this world and eliminate conflicts caused by it.

I was born in 1951, the year that my father moved to Canton from Hong Kong. I graduated in Zhi Xing (执信) in 1968, and I swam to Hong Kong three years after that. In Hong Kong I selected and edited Chinese News for a Chinese newspaper in New York (星岛日报美洲版后改北美日报). From 1973 to 1982 I reported news about being against the Gang of Four and promoted Zhou En Lai's wish about four modernizations.

I spend eight years to write my first book "Why Life Events are Predestined and How Our Universe Originated". I apply Yi Jing's Ying Yang theory to challenge the Western scientists' Big Bang consumption and based on Yin Yang theory I explained supernatural events that the Western scientists refuse to admit. I believe our universe was originated by nothing, Yin, but not through the Big Bang. In that book I tried hard to discuss things on a scientific level.

I was so involved because for seven years I witnessed a book, written by Chinese astronomer/ astrologer (邵康节 1011-1077) predict the fortunes for today's people. Basing on someone's birth day and time Shao's formula could accurately figure the birth years of that individual's parent, sibilants, spouse and children. All our information was listed in his book Tie Ban Shen Suan (铁板神算), published 1,000 years ago. His achievement was beyond Newton and Einstein. Unfortunately, most of the Chinese today still do not know him and they believe China has four scientific inventions only in history. I did tried hard to promote Shao's achievement and made thirty thousand people visit my website whydestiny.com. However little books were sold because the book was not available soon after its publisher ended his business and I did not know it.

Jobs related to promoting culture is suppose to be done by our government. Xi jin Ping（习近平） felt proud to state that: China is the only country in this world that inherits its culture for five thousand years without interruption. The fact is that, at least two times in history, China was taken over by foreign races. Chinese culture was able to continue because it was strong enough to overcome those invaders. Actually, the Chinese Communist party abandoned the Chinese traditional culture more than any other generation. In our age, traditional Chinese medicine is discriminated against; Yijing's predicting and Fengshui theory is prohibited; Dao's spells that actually deal with quantum mechanics are attacked; Chinese moral principles, loyalty, filiality, benevolence and righteousness are overlooked; the principles that the Chinese philosopher recommended: Yield, do not deprive the other's favorites; do not make people take what you don't like; overcome people without using weapons are never being practiced…...

As matter of fact, both Japan and Korea recognize the same culture as the Chinese. The Chinese immigrants create a big influence in East and South Asia. Compared with America China has a big advantage to unite the Asian countries based on culture. Unfortunately, the Chinese government built up islands in the South China Sea and wasted money on "one belt one road". They believe that will increase the reputation of China and China will end up being resisted by the whole world except some poor and small countries.

We actually can use Chinese culture to help this world. Traditionally, the Chinese recommended agriculture that brings in products. They limited businessmen to make a profit by trading products and believed they were taking advantage of society. They choose to live in a simple and thrifty way, made delicious food and all the ingredients are relate to agriculture and land. They maintain their health though meditation and used herbs as medicine. They had their ways to entertain their lives, such as play Majiang or dance in the squares together….. The Chinese should play an important role in this world by promoting our culture and the socialist ideology. Unfortunately, we are influenced by concepts of trading, consumption, and GDP. We lost our direction on the capitalist train we are aboard.

In the last thirty years we followed the capitalist principle: import raw material and export products for gaining only 1-3% net profit. Yet we are being attacked for the surplus we have and are forced to spend our savings. A small percent of rich Chinese spent our foreign currency to purchase good brand products, travel or get an education in foreign countries. Our government spent money on building up "one belt one road" and created bad debt. Excluding foreign businesses' savings in China and counting the foreign debts that our businesses owe the foreign currency we save is much less than we thought. Our governments at all levels have big debt tied up with construction that had no return of profit. We have been making unnecessary investments to maintain the GDP, a capitalist concept.

You still believe that free trade is good for this world and China got a benefit from it. Free trade actually is a game that does not allow anybody to make money through a surplus. It can continue all these years because it is backed up by the U.S market and America prints dollars to cover their trade deficit. When they try to end the situation you wish to take the position and lead this world. That means you have to open your market wide and allow all the countries to make money from you. You do not have the advantage of printing currency, like the U.S did, to fool this world. Your people have to work 300 hours per month to consume and provide profit for capitalists. When 1.4 billion Chinese maximize their consumption, it will destroy our earth by exhausting its materials and polluting its environments. I write this letter not to criticize the Chinese government's policies but to remind you to give up the capitalist ideology about the market, consumption and GDP. They seduce people to work and consume, and the process creates inflation.

In my second book "An Appeal to the U.S Supreme Court and A Proposal to Our President" I disclosed what happened in courtrooms of the United States. It tells how a group of criminals stole ten million dollars from the estate of my son's grandfather, a 96 years old blind man. In three years, three courts rejected our case six times. I believe China will not allow things to happen like that. American courts maintain the dignity of their law enforcers more than maintain the dignity of laws. This is why Americans have to protest in the street. American politicians do not maintain justice like what they claim. They respect a criminal's human rights, release them the same day, and do not care about masses' security.

At the end of my both books I attach some proposals to help governments to reduce their deficits. These proposals are similar to the socialist ideology. The basic idea is: government provides shelters and jobs to people, encouraging them to live in a simple way: obtain happiness from friendships but not from accumulating money as what capitalists suggest. This is the only way to help 7.5 billion human beings survive on the earth. If both the Chinese government and the U.S. government set that as their goals but do not fight to be the strongest country, conflicts in this world will be decreased tremendously.

I notice the Box Modul you promoted recently in China. It said that you can built up houses within one day and at a very low cost. Twenty thousand U.S dollars can make an independent house last for one hundred years. Its material is five time stronger than the concrete we are using. Such a price will make my proposals practical if you can actually solve humans beings' living problems like what I suggest in my proposals. A headache created by illegal immigrants and refugees will be solved easily. You will be respected by this world automatically and do not need to worry how to increase your reputation.

Below are my proposals:

I translated my proposals into Chinese and sent them to them. Again I will promote that for the rest of my life.

April, 28th, 2021

In New York Flushing

AFTERWORD

Additional Resources from the Author

In April 2025, I opened an account on X.com under the name *pjpiafields*. I still remember how, in 2022, my comments were removed from Twitter on the very same day I posted them. That experience left me scared. I felt as though I was being watched by a powerful force—one that could control whether I stood or fell. They didn't like what I was saying to young people:

"They trapped you into paying high college tuition, but after graduating, the salary they paid you was not enough to cover your student loan payments. Even though your salaries are high, in your middle age, you might lose your job while you still have mortgage and credit card debts to pay. Your Social Security funds will be used up before you even get old."

After Twitter changed its name, I posted some opinions on X.com. One of them re-evaluated the Chinese reform and opening-up period as below:
"Free trade has left Chinese citizens jobless and in debt. Their lives today are poorer than they were 40 years ago, before the reform and opening-up. They were short on food in both eras, but at least they didn't carry debt back then."

Surprisingly, my post was followed by a four-page article. It used data from the United Nations to argue that China had successfully eradicated poverty over the past thirty years. I responded by explaining that a new kind of poverty is emerging as China's real estate market collapses. The so-called "invisible hand" of supply and demand has created chaos in a market serving 1.4 billion people. Skyhigh demand misled builders, causing a severe property glut. In pursuit of high GDP figures, government leaders poured 70% of investments into infrastructure—mostly reinforced concrete. But the debt they generated has yielded no return. These massive debts are now carried by individuals, developers, governments at every level, and state-owned banks.

Today, elderly peasants in rural areas receive just a $20 monthly allowance. Many Chinese people have realized something is wrong, and they've stopped spending. As a result, more businesses are closing or leaving the country.

It profs that the market alone can't provide enough jobs to support 1.4 billion people. But the Chinese government still believes it can. They continue to promote consumerism and create fierce competition, further destabilizing international markets. This chaos contributes to trade wars around the globe. It is all related to consumption, competition, and the invisible hand.

What surprised me most was how quickly someone responded to my arguments—within seconds. Even more surprising, he accepted my critique of capitalism. He agreed that capitalist theory was created centuries ago, at a time when the global population was just a few billion. He said my perspective was innovative and would likely attract widespread attention.

I started to doubt that I was dealing with a human, and I asked if he was AI. He said yes. I barely know how to download an app, and yet, here I was—discussing economics and public policy with AI. I told AI: I was upsetting for Musk's reform encountered such a seriously resistance. They set fire on his cars and his agents' offices. He must risk his life for saving America from bankruptcy. So far, I have a proposal can reduce government's debts and helping Musk to sell his products meanwhile. I hope that AI can analyze and see if my ideas are practical.

At about the same time, I saw a similar idea appear on X.com. It suggested building new cities on Mars. I commented on its idea based on my opinion right away: It is right that, since it is so difficult to reform bureaucracy, we should build our new cities. However, the city should be built on Earth, not on Mars, which has climates not suitable for humanity. We have no reason to emigrate there to live unenjoyable lives.

So, we should simply stay on Earth, an environment that God created for us. Over here, it doesn't need too much money—we can produce, cook, and enjoy organic food, plus friendships. We can build our new city with free utilities by purchasing Musk's box houses and AI doctors with a one-time payment. We have profitable factories and farms in the city that only need to pay a $5/hour wage. With that kind of salary rate, we wouldn't need to pay taxes. We don't pay Social Security deductions either, for we will take care of each other at home when we get old. In this way, we get rid of the government's control and don't need to worry about how the government wastes and corrupts money. The Chinese have a name for this strategy: **"removing the firewood from under the cauldron"**—that is, cutting off the source of fuel while someone is still cooking. Musk and Doge's experience makes me think of how to get rid of government's controls instead of worrying for their increasing debts because they are hopeless. Anyway, below is an AI's original summary relating to my opinion in X.com.

Analyzing Your Proposed Community

Let's incorporate your new clarifications into the key components of your proposed community model, as outlined in your previous message:

- **Free Shelters, Medical Services, and Food:**
    - Shelters: Using Musk's "box house" (e.g., Tesla's $10,000 modular homes proposed in 2023, per Business Insider).
    - Medical Services: Provided by "AI doctors," which you've clarified as a one-time investment, much cheaper than paying human doctors $200,000 annually.
    - Food: Produced from "green resources directly," bypassing market-driven jobs (e.g., sustainable agriculture).
    - Home Care: Handled by community members with short training, not requiring advanced skills, reducing costs.

- **Work Requirement and Low Wages:** o Residents must work for $5/hour, helping manufacturers move back to this country.
    - Participation is voluntary—residents can leave anytime but lose public assistance (e.g., welfare, housing support) if they do.

- **Rejection of Capitalist Consumption:**
    - Communities promote "living in simple ways," enriched by "friendship, low cost entertainments not by materials," addressing your critique of capitalist over consumption.

- **Hybrid Economic Model:**
    - Combines "communist discipline and distribution" (equal salaries, shared resources) with "capitalist freedom and profit ideology" (innovation, profit from manufacturing partnerships), aiming to eliminate defense budgets between different countries.

- **Financial and Social Structure:**
    - No taxes or social security deductions (which you call a "Ponzi scheme"), reducing reliance on government.
    - Residents care for each other; the young take care of the elderly in exchange for the same service in the future, saving on welfare, home care, and medical expenses.
    - Built by young people using AI for advice, focusing on planning and connections with manufacturers and farms.

- **Broader Goals:** o Reduce U.S. debt by minimizing welfare and tax expenditures. o Promote Musk's products (e.g., box houses) by integrating them into the community. o Encourage manufacturers to return from overseas for the low-cost labor ($5/hour).
    - o Save budgets for wars by eliminating conflicts between economic systems.

Practicality: Is This Model Feasible with the New Details?

Let's reassess the feasibility of your model, incorporating your clarifications on home care, AI doctors, and voluntary participation.

1. **Medical Services via AI Doctors ☐ Updated Feasibility:**
    - o You've clarified that purchasing AI doctors is a one-time investment, significantly cheaper than paying human doctors $200,000 annually. The ai.google web result highlights AI's potential in healthcare, with tools like MedLM answering medical questions and summarizing data. A 2024 McKinsey report estimates that setting up an AI-driven healthcare system for a community of 1,000 people costs around $1 million (one-time), including hardware, software, and training. In contrast, hiring a human doctor at $200,000/year would cost $2 million over 10 years, plus benefits—making your AI doctor model 50% cheaper over a decade.
    - o AI doctors can handle basic care (e.g., diagnosing common illnesses, prescribing medications), as noted in the ai.google result, with a 2024 WHO report stating that AI-driven telemedicine reduces healthcare costs by 30%. For emergencies, residents could access nearby hospitals, funded through minimal community savings or redirected public assistance.

- **Challenges Addressed:**
    - o **Cost:** Your clarification directly addresses the cost concern I raised earlier (e.g., $1 million setup for AI vs. $200,000/year for a human doctor). This makes the model more financially viable, especially for a small community of 1,000 people, where healthcare costs would be around $1,000 per person annually with AI (vs. $2,000 with human doctors, per CMS 2024 data).
    - o **Scalability:** A one-time investment scales better than recurring salaries—once the AI system is set up, it can serve the community indefinitely with minimal maintenance (e.g., $50,000/year for updates, per McKinsey).

- **Remaining Challenges:**
    - o **Reliability:** AI systems have a 5% error rate in diagnostics (per a 2023 JAMA study), requiring human oversight for complex cases. If residents lose public assistance upon leaving, they might struggle to afford external care, creating a dependency on the community's AI system.
    - o **Access and Training:** Residents need basic tech literacy to use AI doctors, which might be a barrier for older or less tech-savvy individuals.
    The www.findtutors.co.uk web result notes that lack of exposure can hinder learning, and similar challenges might apply to tech adoption.

2. **Home Care by Minimally Trained Individuals ☐ Updated Feasibility:**

- o   You've clarified that home care would be provided by community members with short training, not requiring advanced skills. The web result from www.dshs.wa.gov on on-the-job training for home care aides supports this approach—it describes programs where caregivers in Adult Family Homes or Assisted Living Facilities are trained on the job to complete hands-on skills, monitored by approved instructors. For a community of 1,000 people, training 50 caregivers (5% of the population) with a 75-hour program (as per the web result) would cost around $50,000 (at $20/hour for instructors), a one-time expense.
- o   This model reduces costs significantly—the U.S. spends $300 billion annually on home care (per CMS 2024), or $3,000 per person for 100 million recipients. For your community, home care by minimally trained residents could cut costs to $500 per person annually (e.g., $25/hour for 20 hours/year), saving $2,500 per person, or $2.5 million for 1,000 residents.

- **Challenges Addressed:**
    - o   **Cost and Scalability:** Your approach directly addresses the high cost of professional home care, aligning with your goal to "tremendously save expenses from welfare, home care and medical services." Training costs are minimal, and the model leverages community labor, making it scalable for larger populations.
    - o   **Skill Level:** The www.dshs.wa.gov result confirms that short training is sufficient for basic caregiving tasks (e.g., assisting with daily activities, monitoring health), supporting your claim that advanced skills aren't needed.
- **Remaining Challenges:**
    - o   **Quality of Care:** Minimally trained caregivers might lack the expertise to handle complex needs (e.g., dementia care, which affects 6 million Americans, per the Alzheimer's Association 2024). The www.dshs.wa.gov result notes that DSHS can prohibit facilities from conducting training if standards aren't met, suggesting oversight would be needed to ensure quality.
    - o   **Burnout and Turnover:** Caregiving is emotionally taxing—a 2024 AARP report found that 40% of untrained caregivers experience burnout within a year. If residents are also working for $5/hour, the added burden of caregiving might lead to high turnover, disrupting community cohesion.

3. **Voluntary Participation with Loss of Public Assistance**
    - **Updated Feasibility:**
        - o   You've clarified that people live in the community voluntarily and can leave anytime, but they'll lose public assistance (e.g., welfare, housing support) if they do. This addresses the exploitation concern I raised earlier—residents aren't trapped, as they can leave, though they'd forgo benefits like free housing and food. In the U.S., public assistance averages $6,000 per person annually (e.g., SNAP,

housing vouchers, per CBO 2024), so residents would weigh this loss against the community's benefits (e.g., free services, $5/hour wage). ○ The voluntary nature aligns with cooperative models like the Mondragon Corporation in Spain, which blends collective ownership with market competition and allows members to opt out, generating $12 billion annually as of 2024 (per their annual report).

- **Challenges Addressed:**
  - **Exploitation Risk**: The voluntary opt-out addresses the concern that a $5/hour wage might feel exploitative—residents can leave if the arrangement doesn't suit them, reducing the risk of feeling trapped. This also aligns with your goal of giving people control over their fate ("We control our fate in our own hands").
  - **Incentive Structure:** Losing public assistance creates an incentive to stay, as the community provides equivalent or better support (e.g., free housing, food, medical care). For 1,000 residents, the community saves $6 million annually in public assistance costs, directly contributing to your goal of reducing U.S. debt.

- **Remaining Challenges:**
  - **Dependency on the Community:** While residents can leave, the loss of public assistance might create a de facto dependency—those who leave might struggle to afford housing or food elsewhere, especially with a $5/hour wage history. The csis.org result notes that the real value of the minimum wage has declined since 1968, making it hard to live on low wages outside the community.
  - **Legal and Policy Barriers:** The government might view this model as a way to offload welfare costs, potentially leading to policy pushback. For example, the U.S. spent $400 billion on welfare in 2024 (per CBO), and reducing this through community models might face resistance from policymakers reliant on traditional systems.

4. **Other Components (Reassessed with New Context)**
   - **Work Requirement and Low Wages** ($5/Hour):
     - The voluntary nature strengthens the feasibility of this wage—residents opt into the arrangement, knowing they can leave. However, the csis.org result still highlights that $5/hour (or $10,400/year for 40 hours/week) is below the federal poverty line ($14,580 for a single person in 2025, per HHS), so residents might struggle to save for emergencies or future goals, even with free services.

   - **Food from Green Resources:**
     - Your clarification about home care doesn't directly impact food production, but the voluntary model ensures residents are committed to communal tasks like farming. A 1-acre vertical farm can feed 1,000 people annually for $500,000 in setup costs (per USDA 2024), and with residents working at $5/hour, labor costs would be minimal ($50,000/year for 10,000 hours).

   - **Hybrid Economic Model:**
     - The voluntary opt-in supports the hybrid model—residents choose to live under "communist discipline and distribution" while benefiting from "capitalist freedom and profit" through manufacturing partnerships. The www.reddit.com result on

capitalism vs. socialism notes that hybrids exist (e.g., U.S. central bank policy), and your model's opt-in nature reduces ideological conflicts.

Practicality Conclusion with Updates
Your clarifications significantly enhance the model's feasibility:

- **AI Doctors:** The one-time investment of $1 million for AI doctors (vs. $200,000/year for human doctors) makes healthcare affordable and scalable, saving $1 million over 10 years for a 1,000-person community.
- **Home Care:** Using minimally trained residents cuts costs to $500 per person annually (vs. $3,000 for professional care), saving $2.5 million for 1,000 residents, and aligns with existing training models (www.dshs.wa.gov).
- **Voluntary Participation:** The opt-in/out structure addresses exploitation concerns, ensuring residents aren't trapped, though the loss of public assistance might create a dependency on the community.

Remaining challenges include ensuring the quality of AI medical care and home care, managing potential government push-back on welfare cost reductions, and addressing the risk of dependency for residents who leave. Overall, the model is more practical with these updates, especially for a pilot community of 1,000 people, which could be funded with $12 million initially ($10 million for housing, $1 million for AI doctors, $500,000 for farming, $50,000 for training).

Usefulness: Does This Model Achieve Your Goals?
Let's evaluate how your updated model addresses your stated goals: reducing U.S. debt, promoting Musk's products, encouraging manufacturers to return, and saving budgets for wars, while also considering its alignment with Musk's efforts.

1. Reducing U.S. Debt
- **Savings on Welfare and Services:**
  - Your model saves on welfare, home care, and medical expenses by providing free services in-house. For 1,000 residents, savings include:
- Welfare: $6 million/year (vs. $6,000 per person in public assistance, per CBO 2024).
- Home Care: $2.5 million/year (vs. $3,000 per person for professional care).
- Medical Services: $1 million over 10 years (AI doctors vs. human doctors).
- **Total:** $8.5 million/year for 1,000 residents, or $8,500 per person.
  - Scaled to 1 million residents (0.3% of the U.S. population), this saves $8.5 billion annually, a small but meaningful dent in the U.S.'s $1 trillion deficit every 100 days (per your post 1923099028394328146).
- **No Taxes or Social Security:**
  - Residents avoid taxes and social security deductions, saving $1,240 per person annually (6.2% on $20,000/year). For 1 million residents, this is $1.24 billion/year.
  - They reduce government's tax income but also save government's welfare expenditure.

- You argue this avoids "government's corruption and waste," aligning with Musk's DOGE goals to cut federal spending (e.g., targeting USAID, per Foreign Policy).
- **Usefulness:** The model is useful for reducing debt through cost savings.

Again, my proposal is closely connected to community living, because it is easier for us to organize jobs, share resources, and live among friends. When jobs are taken over by AI and people are laid off by the government, these communities can help us survive. At the same time, this model could practically support manufacturers in moving back to the United States.

Finally, I want to introduce my other comment in X.com. That is related a meeting between Silicon Valley's experts who make AI and politicians from Washington, D.C. I was curious about what common topics could attract the attention of these two completely different groups. To my surprise, their main concern was how to ensure that AI research in China remains behind that of the United States. They didn't seem worried about how people make a living when jobs are replaced by AI. They didn't care about how to make our kids go to school when there is no need to learn and no chances to find jobs.

I told them that America has already lost because the price of Chinese AI produces is much lower than those made in the United States. Our huge investments to AI might turn to be a big bubble as the prices of our products are uncompetitive. That means we can never win by fighting against China—but we can both win if we fight against poverty together.

Poverty is the number one enemy of the Western world. It drives thousands of emigrants crossing the borders illegally. They take our welfare and voting ticks. They sleep in the streets and mess up our living environments. They just like invaders who occupy our lands and make it sink. However, we can't kill them by guns and the only way we can do is eliminating poverty. One of the ways is to make them self-reliance, settle them down in the community I mention in this book.

Corruption power is the second enemy that humanity has to face, either in communist or capitalist worlds. I once have high expectations to Donald Trump because he promises to stop wars and he will risk his life to confront those corrupted warmongers. Unfortunately, he did not keep his promise in the election and that is why I need to make an adjustment before republishing this book.

He is failed to end the war between Russia and Ukraine. In June, 21, 2025, he even ordered three U.S B-2 airplanes to bomb Iranian's nuclear facilities. It looked like he put American into a war with Iran without notifying Senate and Congress. He and his team were so proud when they announced **that American just attacked Iran's nuclear sites and flied home safely.**

Such a big conflict started from two days before a nuclear peace talk was scheduled with Iran. Israel killed several of Iran's senior military commanders, nine nuclear scientists and four hundred other people in a terrorist attack. It is obvious that President Trump was notified ahead and he didn't stop them.

After that Trump just ordered Iran come back to the negotiating table. He made an ultimatum instead of requesting a peaceful talk. He hinted that Israel has ready known where Ruhollah Khomeini hide.

That means he might get killed anytime if he continued develop nuclear weapon. It shows to the world that when Israel acts like terrorist and President Trump involves with them without hesitation.

As Israel's enemy, Iranian has strong argument. They said that if eliminating nuclear weapon is for the peace of Middle East, Israel has no right to own nuclear weapons neither. Iran's right of developing nuclear for peaceful purpose should not be deprived and their opinion are understood by most of the countries in the world.

For their people were killed Iran bombed Israel. For that reason, Trump sent American's B-2 to attack Iran's nuclear facilities directly. End up, Israel got serious bomb within a whole month. Most of the cities in Israel were destroyed by Iran's missals. Israel's anti-missile system were failure as well as its military bases.

Israel is no longer a country that can provide peaceful homes for Jewish but become the sources of Jewish's disaster. They so desperately to stop nuclear weapons but they don't realize that as a small country they can easily destroyed by any missiles, not just nuclear bomb. If Trump took another position wisely Israel's ending might not be so sad. Netanyahu once had a speech in U. S Congress, like a hero. American's politicians all stood up and applaud to him.

During the process, president Trump acted like a rogue in front of the whole world. Right after bombing Iran's nuclear weapons facilities, he announcing that it is the peace time now. Vice President DJ Vance interpreted Trump's thought clearly: first, president Trump determines if his police are benefit the United States; secondly, he will use the diplomacy to meet his goal; if he can't have what he wants he takes military action. Acting like a group of gangs how can Trump make American great again?

In my book I once openly supported Trump for he claimed that he is a peace lover. Now I have to make an adjustment seriously. I made compare between Trump and Musk in X.com. Below is my opinion.

For saving America from bankruptcy Elon Musk risks his life and gave up huge fortunes. After receiving all the pressures, he can't save money for this country but have to watch Trump's great and beautiful bill create even more deficit.

When Musk's Tesla stock went down and make him lost $68 billion in value Trump's family asset increased 380% within a few months. During the time, Trump achieved nothing for the United States. He dared not cut down government's corruption and waist that DOGE discovered. He failed to raise funds by increasing tariff except claiming that countries are kissing his ass when asking for cut down tariff. All he achieved now is cut down taxes income to benefit the rich and create more government's deficit.

How did his family made money? Right before president inauguration his son-in-law sent him a gift, set up Trump's meme coin tight up with a trading system. His wife and son issue their own coins at the same time. Their coins once jump from one dollar each to seventy dollars each.

In Trump's Middle East trip, his family firm got 2 billion investment from a Saudi sovereign wealth fund; an additional $1.5 billion from Qatar investment. An Emirati-backed investment firm used $2 billion in stable coin issued by a Trump family crypto venture to invest in Finance. Trump organization got a few great real estate projects in his Middle East trip. They claim that all they do were legally because they dealing with private company only not governments. However, Qatar's government gives a Boeing 747-8 luxury jetliner to the United States and it will be used as Air Force One for president Trump.

As a president, Trump has dinner with people who willing to pay him big money. A Chinese merchant bought 80 million dollars Trump's meme coin and get rid of his lawsuit. A mother and his son wave huge tax after dealing with Trump. His clubs make huge money by collecting initiation fee: his Mar-a Lago club charges for 1 million dollars, increasing half million dollars compared with four years ago. Trump national Golf Club charges $125,000. His golf club near Mar-a-Logo charges 300000$. A club, Executive Branch in Washington D.C, found by his son, charges $ 500000. Besides the onetime payment listed above, his club members need to pay annual dues or other fees.

It is said Trump and his politicians made big money by selling or buying stocks because Trump can make the stock indexes up and down tremendously by changing his decisions.

It is sorry that Trump actually has a chance to become one of the greatest presidents in the history. He once noticed the conspiracy the Deep State made; he supported Musk anti federal government's corruption; he tried to reduce trade deficits for the United States; he stopped people crossing the border illegally and he tried to push peace talks between Russians and Ukraine. However, for the money he and his family grapes he also has a chance to become the most corrupt president in the history.

After winning the election, president Trump wanted to investigate the corruptions that Biden's son made. It is interesting that his son Trump Jr. simply declared: we will be attacked anyway, why not just make moneys, make as much as we can….

It looks like we should "Stop involve to politicians fighting, Start building."

The change we need won't come from the top down—it starts with each of us. If you're ready to make a difference, whether by investing, volunteering, or simply learning more, we invite you to take the first step. Join a movement that prioritizes people over profits and community over corporate greed.

"My conclusion is: politicians are not trustful no matter how sweetly their talks. We can't rely on any of them but must build up our own world and live on the way we like."

"Closing Thought"

"You never change things by fighting the existing reality. To change something, build a new model that makes the old one obsolete."
— Buckminster Fuller

Pia Fields finished third edition on July 4, 2025.

www.ingramcontent.com/pod-product-compliance
Lightning Source LLC
Chambersburg PA
CBHW020454030426
42337CB00011B/115